Morgan Jones

Man of Conscience

Wayne David

welsh academic press

Cardiff

Published in Wales by Welsh Academic Press, an imprint of

Ashley Drake Publishing Ltd
PO Box 733
Cardiff
CF14 7ZY

www.welsh-academic-press.wales

First Edition – 2019

ISBN
Paperback – 978 1 86057 1411

British Library Cataloguing-in-Publication Data.
A CIP catalogue for this book is available from the British Library.

Typeset by Prepress Plus, India (www.prepressplus.in)
Printed by Akcent Media, Czech Republic

CONTENTS

Introduction   v
Foreword by Hilary Benn MP   vii
Glossary   xi

1.   The Early Years   1
2.   Opposition to the First World War   7
3.   The Caerphilly By-election of 1921   29
4.   MP and Education Minister   43
5.   Westminster and Wales   65
6.   The Internationalist   75
7.   The West Indies and the Last Year   92

Epilogue   106

Index   109

Select Bibliography   113

To Jayne, without whose encouragement this book would never have been written.

INTRODUCTION

If ever there was a 'Labour of Love' then this book is it. In December 2014, in the knowledge that Morgan Jones had been a conscientious objector in the First World War, the Speaker of the House of Commons asked me to deliver a lecture on the former Caerphilly MP in the Speaker's House. In preparing that lecture I realised that my subject was far more interesting and noteworthy than I had at first realised. Here was a man whose name, what he stood for and what he achieved, deserves to be known far and wide.

Following that lecture, and encouragement from friends and colleagues, I decided to extend my research and prepare a concise biography of this exceptional man. Sources of information were disparate, although I was lucky in having as my starting point a private and unpublished life-story of Morgan Jones written by the late John Sheaff, the husband of Jones' daughter, Margaret. Sadly, Margaret, has recently passed away but I was fortunate to have gathered her recollections and a number of her photographs and items of memorabilia a couple of years ago which are reproduced in this book. Providing huge support at all times was Margaret's son Nick, who gave me enormous encouragement and urged me on even when I was overloaded with my own political activities.

I owe a huge debt to the staff in a number of libraries and archives in Caerphilly, Bargoed, Cardiff, Swansea, Aberystwyth, Manchester and London, and my gratitude must also go to all those friends and acquaintances who gave me nuggets of valuable information. Special thanks must go to my good friend and colleague, Nick Thomas-Symonds MP. As an accomplished historian, Nick gave me invaluable advice, for which I am extremely appreciative.

Soon after I had started my research for the book I was invited to Margaret and John's home in Bath. We had a memorable lunch and I recall being told at the end of the meal that the cutlery we had just used had been given to Morgan Jones and his wife as a wedding present by the Parliamentary Labour Party. From that moment on I felt that I was really getting to know Morgan Jones. Little did I think that before long I would be getting married myself and thanking my wife for her support in helping me write this book, but I am and I do, because without Jayne's support I doubt that this book would have seen the light of day.

I also want to thank the people of the Caerphilly constituency who have shown such an interest in this project. If it belongs to anyone, this book belongs to the electors of the Caerphilly constituency who Morgan Jones represented for nearly two decades.

Last but by no means least, my sincere thanks go to my dedicated staff, especially Chris Bradley whose quiet forbearance helped me to transform an idea into a book.

Wayne David MP
Caerphilly
April 2019

FOREWORD

Wayne David has done us all a great service in writing such a readable and interesting book about the life of Morgan Jones.

Jones was a man of principle and pragmatism whose story in many ways reflects the journey of the Labour Party during its life thus far.

Born in the Rhymney Valley in 1885, Jones came of age at a time of social and political turmoil. A student contemporary of his described him as 'an enthusiast in all things political, with a burning desire to better the underdog.' It was a description that presciently reflected what Jones did in the rest of his all too short, but very full, life.

Inspired by his politics and his faith, and propelled onwards by his capacity for sheer hard work, Morgan Jones joined the Independent Labour Party and preached its values.

Those values were soon to be tested, and Wayne David's book really brings to life the impact that the First World War and his refusal to be conscripted had on Jones. The struggle to hold to his principles resulted in both physical and mental hardship – he was imprisoned several times – and scathing criticism from those, including in his own community, who regarded conscientious objectors as the lowest of the low. It took enormous courage to stand up for what he believed in, but having inherited his pacifism from his mother, Jones' utter conviction was that the war was unjustified, unnecessary and set worker against worker.

At the time, as expertly explained by the author, there was a divide between the absolutist objectors (who refused to do anything in support of the war effort) and the alternativists (who would not serve on the front line but would do other work), and we learn how Jones wrestled with the two options available to him.

After the war he continued his work as a councillor and put his prodigious effort into improving housing and the lives of those he represented. In 1921, Jones was selected as the Labour candidate for Caerphilly, and this book delights in its description of the cut and thrust of the campaign in which the Communist Party (CP) was a noisy opponent – a reminder of the radical politics of the time.

The communists wanted revolution but Morgan Jones believed in evolution. On polling day, the evolutionary won out over both the revolutionary and the status quo when he beat the Communist and the National Liberal – his main opponent – to achieve a majority of 4,741. *The Times* described the result as a 'sweeping triumph for the Labour candidate.'

Unlike some early Labour MPs who regarded Westminster as a place for occasional appearances rather the main focus of their work, Morgan Jones moved his family to London because he believed the role required total commitment to parliament. His maiden speech revealed his preacher's passion for justice and equality, ending it with a stirring appeal to the government "to do something, and that speedily, to bring some comfort, some contentment to the homes of the common people, that they may feel once more proud of their native land." It was a cause that marked out the whole of his political life.

During this time, Jones had to devote a lot of effort to dealing with the problems created by the Communist Party, and its attempts at infiltration and its criticisms of him personally – a reminder that radical politics can all too easily be consumed by hunting traitors rather than defeating Tories.

His range of interests and speeches was astonishingly wide – international development, school meals, self-government for the colonies, nationalisation of the coal industry, support for a Jewish state – but his priority was education. He quickly became a Labour education spokesperson and there is more than a contemporary ring to his contributions when he spoke about the need to protect school funding from cuts and austerity.

Having served as deputy secretary to the Board of Education in Ramsay MacDonald short lived Labour Government in 1924, Jones returned in the same post in 1929 when Labour formed its first majority administration. David argues that although MacDonald's record on education 'was not at all positive' – two flagship education bills failed to progress – Jones played a significant role in developing the party's educational thinking.

In opposition again, having comfortably retained his seat despite the disastrous result for Labour in the 1931 general election, Jones served as Labour's education spokesman. His proposal for free secondary education would have encouraged working class families to keep their children in school and Jones was one of the earliest voices behind Labour's eventual commitment to the comprehensive ideal. In June 1935, Jones first proposed a secondary school 'so big that the practically-minded children and the academically-minded children will go through the same portals', and he helped lay the early foundations of the post-war consensus though his participation in the Education Advisory Committee alongside R.H. Tawney, Barbara Drake and Brian Simon. Jones believed passionately in education as the means of improving the lives of his constituents.

Throughout his life, Jones was a caring and formidable advocate for the community he was born in and represented. As a patriotic Welshman he also loved his country, was an early advocate of devolution and in June 1938 led a delegation of the Welsh parliamentary party to 10 Downing Street to try and persuade Prime Minister Neville Chamberlain of the case for a Welsh secretary of state in the cabinet. Chamberlain was unmoved, but the seed was sown and 26 years later James Griffiths became the first occupant of the post.

Jones was a parliamentary reformer. As chairman of the Committee of Public Accounts he tackled a loophole that allowed governments to avoid obtaining parliamentary approval for areas of expenditure by introducing the 1932 Committee of Public Accounts 'Concordat'. It endures to this day.

The latter part of this excellent book explains with great insight how Jones' attitude to international relations and conflict evolved during the 1930s, a decade famous for its turmoil and isolationism. In his maiden speech at the 1932 Inter-Parliamentary Union conference in Geneva, Jones called for peace and disarmament, and for reconciliation to take precedence over revenge, but he also saw democratic values being subverted by authoritarianism and urged politicians to act in a way that upheld trust in representative democracy. The parallels with the present day are striking.

This experience shaped Jones' transition from pacifism to support for peacekeeping though the League of Nations. At the time, Labour began to adopt a more pragmatic view of international relations, and Jones spoke out against the Luftwaffe's bombing of Guernica in Spain and highlighted the terrible humanitarian consequences. David illuminates how the Spanish Civil War changed Jones' own personal beliefs, and how he became increasingly concerned with the treatment of the Jewish community in Nazi Germany.

The defining internal debate of his life came to the fore in the article he wrote, aptly titled 'Perplexities of a Pacifist'. Looking at what was happening all around him, Jones concluded that collective security had to be supported against international 'gangsters' so as to defend the rule of international law and the League of Nations. His pacifist convictions, shaped by his unique combination of principle and pragmatism, had now changed.

Morgan Jones' untimely death in 1939 deprived his constituents of an outstanding representative and the Labour Party of one of its brightest lights.

In so many ways Wayne David's book, which deserves to be widely read, brings out the importance of conviction and belief as the driving force in politics. Moreover, just as Morgan Jones' ideas and beliefs were shaped by the struggle between principle and pragmatism, so the same choices and dilemmas confront Labour in the modern era.

As our movement's history, and Morgan Jones' extraordinary life, teach us, it is when we combine the two that we are able to change the world. His friend and colleague, Rhys J. Davies MP, said of him that he was a "man of upright character … immersed in spiritual values … and he never forgot the deeper social problems that in the end determine the destinies of nations."

What a fine and fitting tribute to a life that was well lived.

Hilary Benn MP
Westminster
April 2019

GLOSSARY

CWB: Central Welsh Board
CO: Conscientious Objector
CP: Communist Party
CPGB: Community Party of Great Britain
EAC: Education Advisory Committee
'Fed': South Wales Miners' Federation
IFTU: International Federation of Trade Unionists
ILP: Independent Labour Party
IPU: Inter-Parliamentary Union
MFGB: Miners' Federation of Great Britain
NALT: National Association of Labour Teachers
NCF: No-Conscription Fellowship
NCLC: National Council of Labour Colleges
NEC: National Executive Committee
NFRB: New Fabian Research Bureau
PLP: Parliamentary Labour Party
SWACC: South Wales Anti-Conscription Council
SWMF: South Wales Miners' Federation
TLL: Teachers' Labour League
TUC: Trades Union Congress
UDC: Urban District Council
WEA: Workers' Educational Association
WNCE: Welsh National Council for Education

1

The Early Years

Morgan Jones was born in the small Rhymney Valley village of Gelligaer, Glamorgan, on May 3rd, 1885, in the modest Rhos Cottages, and in the shadow of the ancient parish church of St Catwg at the foot of Gelligaer mountain.[1]

Gelligaer is a community with a long history, extending far back before the construction of an important Roman fort. From the middle of the 19th century however, Gelligaer was dominated by the mining industry and Morgan Jones' father, Elias, was a hard-working 'quiet and unobtrusive'[2] coal miner whose family had come from the Bedwas area in the lower Rhymney Valley. Jones' mother, Sarah Ann, was from the nearby village of Llanfabon and was reputed to have been a servant in the nearby Tudor manor of Llancaiach Fawr. What is certain, however, is that her life was far from easy, with her family chores including the rearing and tending of the livestock.[3]

Although Sarah Ann was illiterate, she was extremely ambitious for her children, especially the boys. Morgan Jones was the fifth of seven children – five sons and two daughters – and his ability was quickly recognised by Sarah Ann who gave him particular attention and encouragement.[4] Indeed, throughout Jones' life, Sarah Ann was to give him unfailing support.

Welsh was the language of the hearth, and the family were devout non-conformists with Sarah Ann a member of the congregation at the local Welsh-language Baptist chapel.[5] Politically, Morgan Jones' family had few overt affiliations but their sympathy – as shared across the south Wales coalfield – was almost certainly with the Liberals and, as a result of this upbringing, his commitment to non-conformity, his love of the Welsh language, and his support for temperance[6] were to remain with him throughout his life.

The young Morgan Jones received his education at Gelligaer and Hengoed Elementary Schools before entering Lewis School, Pengam in 1897 'at the head of the list of Scholarship winners'.[7] The school was once supposedly described by Lloyd George as the 'Eton of the valleys' and over the years it saw a number of its pupils achieve distinction. Amongst its luminaries was

The Jones family home in Gelligaer. (Courtesy of Nick Sheaff)

Thomas Jones (or T J as he was known), who attended Lewis School a few years before Morgan Jones and rose to become assistant cabinet secretary to Lloyd George.[8]

After matriculating from Lewis School in 1901, Jones began training as a pupil teacher at Gilfach Fargoed Boys' School, Bargoed, where his head teacher commented that he showed 'skill, aptitude and fondness for his work'.[9] On his advice, Jones applied for, and gained admission to University College, Reading where he read for an Arts degree, although it is unclear whether he actually graduated. After university, he went on to train to be a teacher in Reading Normal Training College. While at Reading University, Jones was elected President of the Men's Student Union, known as 'Shells', and formed a Sunday afternoon students' group which debated a range of economic and political issues. A fellow student described him as 'an enthusiast in all things political, with a burning desire to better the underdog'.[10] Morgan Jones' religious conviction also saw him become a regular preacher in the Baptist chapels around Berkshire.[11]

In 1907, Morgan Jones returned to Gilfach Boys' School as a qualified teacher and remained there until he transferred to Bargoed Boys' School in June 1914. He was also elected President of the Glamorgan Federation of Teachers. At the same time, he became a regular Baptist lay preacher in chapels throughout the upper Rhymney Valley.[12]

By this time, with his religious convictions already firmly held, Jones' political views had developed substantially. Leaving behind his initial Liberal leanings, he returned to the Rhymney Valley a convinced socialist and, in 1908, joined the Independent Labour Party (ILP), helping to establish the party's first branch in the valley.[13]

At the turn of 20th century, right across the south Wales coalfield, Liberalism and its working class variant, Lib-Labism, were being questioned by more radical political creeds. The ILP, with its materialist analysis and its progressive morality, was at the cutting edge of the challenge and, in so many ways, Morgan Jones personified the new left-of-centre political consensus which

A student at Reading University, circa 1907. (Courtesy of Nick Sheaff)

was beginning to emerge in industrial Wales. Soon, Morgan Jones was in demand as a speaker for the ILP,[14] and his pulpit skills along with his school teaching experience, helped him establish a reputation as one of the party's most effective platform speakers: his speeches being always well-prepared, crystal clear, succinct and spiced with humour.

Although drawn to the big political questions of the day, it was at the local level that Morgan Jones made his initial political impact when, in March 1911, he decided to stand for election to his local council, Gelligaer Urban District Council (UDC).[15] Morgan Jones' parents had by now moved to Bargoed and, as he was still living at the family home, the young radical decided to stand as a socialist for one of the two seats in the Bargoed ward. The other two candidates were the incumbent Edward Lewis, a local Conservative businessman, and E. Jones, who stood as a Labour candidate. There is no account of the election campaign but it is fair to assume that Jones gave it his all: he needed to as he only defeated Edward Lewis by a mere 11 votes.[16]

Morgan Jones soon became a popular and hard-working councillor, as confirmed just two months after his election by a reporter from the local newspaper, the *Caerphilly Journal*, who, having been with Jones in Bargoed, observed that 'Mr Morgan Jones will have a lot of questions to ask and complaints to make at the next meeting of the Gelligaer Council judging by the way he is button-holed in the street by his constituents'.[17]

At that time, Gelligaer UDC did not have a political group structure as such and it seems to have functioned on a largely apolitical, consensual basis without any firm political leadership. Jones' election introduced a new dynamic to the authority and he was undoubtedly a breath of fresh air on the council, with a wide range of issues immediately grabbing his attention. Seeking real change, and quickly, Jones had no time for vacillation and indecision and he soon became the council's 'leading light'. Indeed, it is clear from the council minutes that Morgan Jones was soon the authority's most active councillor.[18] At one council meeting, he successfully moved no fewer than six resolutions, ranging from protesting to the local railway company about overcrowding and the 'filthy conditions of the railway carriages', to demanding that the clerk prepare a report on the rates of pay of the labourers working for the council, with a view to those rates being increased. Other issues which received Jones' attention included the progress towards completing the new Isolation Hospital at Pengam, the poor state of street lighting, the inadequacy of public urinals and the need to improve the sewage system in the area.[19]

The First World War, however, created a painful hiatus in Jones' work on the council. This was especially the case after January 1916 when the local authority was drawn into the government's efforts to enforce conscription and Morgan Jones was incarcerated. After the war, and when he was finally released from military detention, Jones quickly resumed his council work.

In the aftermath of the Great War, Morgan Jones was very aware of the increasing economic problems which were now impacting on the Rhymney Valley. In 1921 there was a protracted lock-out in the coal industry and unemployment was increasing rapidly. There was, of course, little the local authority could do to tackle the macro-economic problems of the area but he gave his full support to the significant efforts the council made to alleviate suffering. Importantly, Jones was an active member of the council's Local Relief Committee.[20]

It was, however, housing which was Morgan Jones' main and consistent concern as a Gelligaer councillor. Within weeks of his election in 1911, he successfully moved a resolution on housing which in time was to have a massive impact on housing provision throughout the district. The resolution referred to the failure of 'private enterprise' to provide homes at a 'sufficiently low rental to meet the requirements of a mining district'. It also called for the creation of a committee of the whole council to 'deal with the matter'.[21]

The lack of adequate and affordable housing in the Rhymney Valley had become a huge issue and, in October 1914, Jones drew attention to the fact that overcrowding was "rampant"[22] in the Bargoed area, referring to a case he knew of a young married couple who needed a house. In a council meeting (and elaborated in a letter to the local newspaper) Jones stated that £1 in 'key money' (the deposit) had been agreed but the property had then been given to an applicant who had offered 25 shillings. Such practice, he said, was widespread and local government needed to take a lead in tackling the situation.[23]

With the rapid growth of the coal industry, the population of the Gelligaer UDC area had doubled in just 10 years, and not only was there a lack of affordable housing, much of the housing was 'unfit for human habitation'.[24] Although a 'special' housing committee was established – rather than the council as a whole dealing with the issue – Jones was appointed its chairman and soon the local authority was looking at purchasing land for the building of council houses. Initially, the first priority was to

Sarah Ann, Morgan Jones' mother, circa 1900. (Courtesy of Nick Sheaff)

build houses at Pontlottyn, where the housing situation was particularly bad, but before long the council's ambitions grew as it became clear that there was a huge need for good quality housing throughout the district.[25]

With Morgan Jones as chairman of the housing committee, in 1920-21, Gelligaer UDC built dozens of council houses and was in the process of purchasing land for further houses in the villages of Pengam, Bedlinog, Fochriw, Deri and Trelewis,[26] but it was in the town of Bargoed that the council's success was greatest. Here, in April 1921, the housing committee reported to the full council that land had been acquired at Heol Ddu Isaf, that the first houses of an anticipated total of 800 would be completed within weeks, and further development in the area was anticipated.[27]

This was 'municipal socialism' in practice, with Morgan Jones as one of its principal standard bearers, and those council-built houses are still amongst the best of their kind in south Wales.

Although he was elected to Glamorgan County Council in December 1919, immediately becoming a member of its education committee, Gelligaer UDC remained the main focus for Jones' local government interests, and largely because of his hard work and leadership, Gelligaer UDC succeeded in improving the quality of life of thousands of people. What is more, this was achieved at a time of growing economic dislocation and social hardship. The council's housing policy in particular was both radical and innovative, and it established Gelligaer UDC as one of the most far-sighted local authorities in Wales.

Notes

1. John Sheaff, *Morgan Jones – a Memorial*, (unpublished, 1986), p.1.
2. *Merthyr Pioneer*, January 15th, 1916.
3. John Sheaff, op. cit., p.4.
4. Ibid.
5. *Western Mail*, April 26th, 1939.
6. *South Wales Echo*, April 24th, 1939.
7. Dylan Rees, 'Morgan Jones: Educationalist and Labour Politician', *Morgannwg: The Journal of Glamorgan History* (Vol. XXX1), 1987, p.66.
8. See Chris Williams, *Oxford Dictionary of National Biography*, Oxford University Press, 2004.
9. See Thomas Jones, *Rhymney Memories*, (Gwasg Gomer, 1970).
10. *Berkshire Chronicle*, April 28th, 1939.
11. Dylan Rees, *Dictionary of Labour Biography*, J. Bellamy and J. Saville (Eds.), Vol. IX, (Palgrave Macmillan, 1993), p.146.
12. Ibid.
13. Ibid.
14. Ibid.
15. *Bargoed Journal*, March 2nd, 1911.
16. *Bargoed Journal*, March 30th, 1911.
17. *Caerphilly Journal*, May 25th, 1911.
18. Minutes of Gelligaer Urban District Council, UDG/C/1/3 – UDG/C/1/11, Glamorgan Archives.
19. Minutes of Gelligaer Urban District Council, UDG/C/1/4, op. cit.
20. Minutes of Gelligaer Urban District Council, UDG/C/1/16, op. cit.
21. Minutes of Gelligaer Urban District Council, UDG/C/1/3, op. cit.
22. *Merthyr Express*, October 10th, 1914.
23. *Merthyr Express*, November 9th, 1914.
24. Minutes of Gelligaer Urban District Council, UDG/C/1/15, op. cit.
25. Ibid.
26. Ibid.
27. Minutes of Gelligaer Urban District Council, UDC/C/1/16, op. cit.

2

Opposition to the First World War

While local government was hugely important to the young Morgan Jones, it was the First World War which fundamentally changed his life. From the moment Britain declared war on Germany in August 1914, Jones was a vocal opponent. Like many in the ILP, he believed that the war was unjustified and unnecessary – an imperialist conflict which set worker against worker – so as a socialist and an internationalist, he staunchly opposed the conflict on political grounds.

Morgan Jones also adopted a Christian pacifist position and declared his opposition to all forms of warfare, believing that the destruction of human life should not be a means of solving international disagreements.[1] Jones attributed his strong pacifist views to his mother, saying that she had taught

Soldiers outside the recruitment office in Bargoed. (Courtesy of Paul James)

him 'from the cradle' to be a pacifist and he appreciated her theology even more than that of the churches.[2]

Jones' unequivocal views led him in the direction of like-minded individuals, notably Fenner Brockway and Bertrand Russell, and when the No-Conscription Fellowship (NCF) was formed late in 1914, Morgan Jones soon joined and was appointed to its national committee. He was given responsibility for cases in south Wales and later became the chairman of the South Wales Anti-Conscription Council.[3] For a short time, he also worked at the NCF's offices in London.[4]

When war was declared a huge wave of jingoism had swept across the country and many confidently expected the war to be over by Christmas. Wales was a particularly important recruiting ground for the armed forces, particularly after the leadership of the 'Fed' – The South Wales Miners' Federation – gave fulsome support to the war effort. Miners' leaders like William Brace and Tom Richards were frequent speakers at recruitment meetings across the coalfield, and the response in the Rhymney Valley was as enthusiastic as anywhere. In Jones' home town of Bargoed, the first three months of the war saw a reported 1,315 men recruited at the Labour Exchange.[5]

In the surrounding colliery villages it was a similar story; in Maesycwmmer it was reported that there were 141 recruits during the first week of September; in Pengam 'about 100 men' were recruited; and in Hengoed 30 to 40 recruits were accompanied by a band and a large crowd of well-wishers to the local railway station.[6]

Further down the valley, the enthusiasm for the war was no less marked. In Caerphilly, the local newspaper proudly announced in mid-September that, 'The locality has done remarkably well as regards recruiting and over 600 have been enlisted'.[7] Even in the Aber Valley, which saw the loss of 440 men in an appalling colliery explosion in Senghenydd only a year earlier, the local pro-war Labour MP, Alfred Onions, went on a public platform and said that he hoped there would be a good number of recruits from the valley despite the losses in the explosion. He told a recruitment meeting in Abertridwr that he had seen a number of young men in the village square and they should be encouraged to do their patriotic duty.[8] Onions was not to be disappointed; by the middle of November 1914 there were 680 recruits from the Aber Valley villages of Senghenydd and Abertridwr.[9]

All sections of the community demonstrated their patriotism. In churches, chapels, public houses and concert halls people enthusiastically supported the war effort. Dozens of well-attended concerts were soon being organised across the length and breadth of the Rhymney Valley and the funds raised at these events were put to effective use.[10] In the lower part of the valley, the monies raised helped to house dozens of Belgian refugees who had been displaced by the invading German army.[11] Lloyd George had forcefully drawn parallels between Wales and Belgium as comparable small nations and many felt it was their duty to show solidarity. The monies from these concerts were also used to 'reduce distress' for those in the community who had lost loved ones in the war and were now facing financial hardship.[12]

Soon after the war started, the Red Cross Society held a meeting at The Twyn, in the centre of Caerphilly, to recruit new members to the society.[13] A month later, the Caerphilly Silver Band marched through the town to raise funds for the conversion of a house into a hospital for the war wounded.[14]

In such an atmosphere it was virtually impossible for anyone who opposed, or even questioned the war, to gain a hearing. Keir Hardie, the ILP MP for Merthyr and Aberdare, was 'howled down' at Aberdare Market Hall and in the early part of the war most political opponents of the conflict, including Morgan Jones, kept a relatively low profile.[15]

The surge of enthusiasm for the war, however, was not sustained. The early optimism that the war would be over quickly gave way to a sullen realisation that the war was going to be protracted and bloody. As the conflict went into its second year, the local newspapers carried fewer and fewer reports of patriotic concerts and more reports, often accompanied with photographs, of local men who had been lost in action.[16]

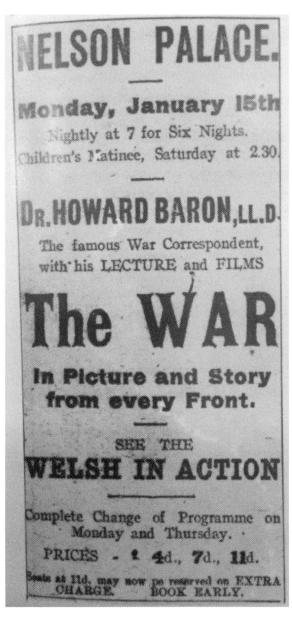

Advertisement from the Merthyr Express, January 1917.

Enthusiastic fundraising for the war effort in Trafalgar Square, Bargoed, circa 1917. (Courtesy of Paul James)

Until 1916, the British army consisted entirely of volunteers, with many joining in response to the famous demonstrative poster of Lord Kitchener which powerfully proclaimed 'Britons. Kitchener Wants You'. But during the course of 1915, as the casualties were mounting, the government felt it necessary to introduce the so-called 'Derby Scheme' to boost recruitment. Despite representations at a local level to Caerphilly UDC, from the MP for Bedwellty, Charles Edwards, and local miners' leaders, for a huge recruitment effort to be made, the scheme locally, as well as across Britain, failed to produce the desired number of recruits.[17] With British casualties at over half a million by the end of 1915, the government decided that it needed to adopt a new approach.

The response of the government was to introduce conscription via the Military Service Act. From January 1916 all unmarried men between the ages of 18 and 41 were regarded as being enlisted in the armed forces, irrespective of whether they had received call-up papers, and military law was to apply to all such men, even if they were still at home. In May 1916, these measures were extended to cover married men as well.

As preparations were made for the introduction of conscription, the campaigns of the NCF and ILP stepped-up a gear and Morgan Jones took the lead in urging opposition to both the war and conscription. He spoke at meetings throughout south Wales and, despite a sore throat which his doctor said needed rest, Morgan Jones delivered a number of stirring addresses.[18] One of his most powerful speeches was delivered at the ILP's Welsh divisional conference in Merthyr, in January 1916. Presiding over the conference as its chairman, Jones told the assembled delegates:

A meeting of the National Executive of the No-Conscription Fellowship, May 1916. Morgan Jones is standing, second from left.

"The lust for blood still remains apparently unsatisfied. The sacrifice of life and treasure, so unprecedented in character, absolutely unparalleled in history, still goes on. Meaningless words and phrases are still successfully used to delude the innocent and to trip the unwary among the workers of the belligerent nations. Theirs' not to reason why, theirs' but to do and die…But in common with a few stalwart comrades in other lands, whose untiring efforts on behalf of peace, in face of almost insuperable obstacles we whole-heartedly acknowledge we are proud to rally round the Flag of the Old International, and proclaim anew the solidarity of the workers of the world."[19]

As his speech reached its climax, Jones rousingly declared:

"Let reactionists of all parties coalesce if they will; our fight is not with persons: we fight with the principle and spirit of reaction itself. It has chosen to throw down the gauntlet, and the ILP, without regret and without hesitancy, take up the challenge, and with courage and determination the battle shall be fought in parliament, and in the mine, factory and workshop. Let there be no mistake about it, the ILP and all it stands for, is winning. It shall win in the end. Democracy must prevail. In that spirit, the spirit of the old pioneers and the martyrs of the past, with the same measure of courage and determination that our wonderful party has demonstrated in the past 18 months, let us enter that now draws upon us…we are ready for the fray. We look to the future with hope, but our watchword is still the same as it was of old. We enlist whole-heartedly under the flag of Socialism and international peace".[20]

Under the Military Service Act, local Military Service Tribunals were established to determine cases of exemption for men who could best contribute to the war effort by continuing in their civilian roles, and if a decision was disputed, the Appeals Tribunals and Central Appeal Tribunals were established. Where an individual was applying for exemption from military service on grounds of conscience, however, it was only possible for this to be granted for combatant service but then only when the applicant was engaged in work of national importance. The Act also stated that the death penalty could not be applied to conscientious objectors (COs), although penal measures could.

The effect of this Act was to create two different kinds of conscientious objectors – the 'absolutists' and the 'alternativists'. The absolutists were those who adopted a maximalist position of not only opposing the war but also refusing to accept any kind of alternative work. Most of the 'absolutists' were sent to army camps and/or prison, and were forced to do various kinds of labouring, including 'hard labour'. When incarcerated the absolutists were often subjected to harsh treatment and many had to endure atrocious conditions.

The other kind of conscientious objectors were the 'alternativists'. These were individuals who were wholly opposed to the war but who were prepared to accept some form of alternative employment, mostly in transport or mining. Some alternativists were, however, obliged to be stretcher bearers on the front line, one of the most dangerous occupations of all. Others later accepted a scheme established by the Home Office which offered a modified prison sentence, including some forms of work for those who initially refused any of the types of work set out in the Military Service Act.

Early in 1916, Jones received his call-up papers.[21] At about the same time, Gelligaer UDC was informed that it would be expected to appoint a local tribunal 'to deal with exceptions' under the Military Service Act.[22] At a full council meeting in February 1916, at which Morgan Jones was present, the councillors voted – by only ten votes to eight – to empower the chairman and the clerk to convene a special council meeting whenever necessary to respond to the government's diktat.[23] Such a meeting was convened soon after, but it was inquorate; the Labour members probably having made a deliberate decision not to attend. To circumvent this impasse, those councillors in attendance decided to form themselves into a further 'committee', which then established a local tribunal. It was agreed that this would consist of half a dozen councillors, augmented by a local doctor and a Justice of the Peace.[24]

It was before this local tribunal that Jones duly appeared following his refusal to join the armed forces. After the war, the government ordered that virtually all records relating to the war be destroyed so the minutes of the Gelligaer Military Service Tribunal and the minutes of Gelligaer UDC for this period are

Crowds gather for a military parade in Bargoed, which included a tank that can be seen behind the trees, circa 1917. (Courtesy of Paul James)

not available. Fortunately though, we have reports in the local press and they show that he gave a robust account of himself in front of the tribunal.[25]

Before a packed council chamber in Hengoed, the tribunal chairman read out a statement from Jones, in his presence, which claimed that he was requesting 'Absolute Exemption' on two grounds: as a socialist and internationalist. Morgan Jones believed that all war was wrong as a means of solving international difficulties and disagreements, and secondly it was stated that he was opposed to the current war in particular because he believed that Britain's entry into the war was 'entirely unwarrantable and without justification'.[26]

After the statement had been read out, Jones was asked by the chairman if he had any supplementary statement to make. He responded in the affirmative and proceeded to elaborate on his written statement, but no sooner had he begun, the chairman interrupted and told Jones that he could not introduce "new facts". There then followed a prolonged wrangle lasting 15 minutes between Jones and the chairman during which Jones stressed that he was not a "shirker". This eventually led to a question and answer exchange with members of the tribunal. The questions were varied and ranged from those which asked Jones about his personal beliefs to those which queried his views on foreign policy. As he probably expected, there were also questions about his attitude to

Nurses and soldiers outside the Hanbury Cinema, Bargoed. (Courtsey Paul James)

Germans and how he would respond if a German attacked a friend of his. Jones answered this and other questions without difficulty, but one of the most tricky questions came from the local miners' agent, who asked whether it was the case that not all socialists were opposed to the war. Jones responded that this was of course the case, but it did not alter the strength of his own convictions.[27]

Jones answered all the questions put to him with confidence and eloquence, drawing ripples of applause from his supporters in the public gallery. As well as answering the specific questions, he was also able to make the point towards the end of his appearance that, in his view, the war was the result of "a number of years of wrong-headed diplomacy".[28]

The last question to Jones was put by the chairman: "Since you are not prepared to contribute to the defence of your country in a time of war, I ask you what sacrifice you are prepared to make for your conscience". The tension was palpable as Jones broke the silence that had descended on the tribunal, replying, "[if] I am called upon to give up my own life, I am prepared that that should be taken".[29]

After the hearing, the tribunal withdrew to consider its verdict, not that there was ever any doubt as to what the decision would be. Jones was exempted from combatant service but not from 'alternative work', and as he had refused to undertake 'alternative work', he would face imprisonment.[30]

Following an unsuccessful appeal to an Appeals Tribunal in Cardiff, at 8.30 am on May 29th, 1916, Morgan Jones was arrested at his parents' home – 21 Park Crescent, Bargoed – by the local police inspector. In a letter to Clifford Allen, the chairman of the NCF, Jones wrote that the police officer was 'most courteous and polite' when he called, although his mother 'was somewhat alarmed' by the police officer's arrival. He told Clifford Allen that he had not shown 'the slightest perturbation', explaining that he was already dressed, and about to leave for Abercynon to deal with a case on behalf of the NCF,[31] when the police inspector called to take him to the cells in Bargoed police station.[32]

Later that day the police raided the offices of the ILP at 57 Hanbury Road, Bargoed, but Jones was confident that the police would not have found anything incriminating, although the police did take away a large amount of ILP literature. After the police raid, the secretary of the local ILP branch wryly commented that the local police superintendent would be eligible for membership of the ILP after 'wading through that lot'.[33] A couple of months later, the local magistrates ordered that the seized pamphlets should be destroyed.[34]

Following his arrest, Jones appeared before Cardiff Magistrates Court, where he was fined two shillings and sentenced to four months imprisonment for refusing to obey military orders.[35]

While Morgan Jones was the subject of police action in Wales, the leadership of the NCF was also facing a crackdown in London. At the same time as he was arrested in Bargoed, under the Defence of the Realm Act, other members of the NCF national committee were appearing before magistrates at the unusual venue of the Mansion House, next to the Lord Mayor of London's residence. Eight members of the national committee, including Morgan Jones, were charged with prejudicing recruitment and military discipline by circulating a leaflet which urged the repeal of the Military Service Act.[36] The text of the leaflet was as follows:

Repeal the Act

Fellow citizens:

Conscription is now law in this country of free traditions. Our hard-won liberties have been violated. Conscription means the desecration of principles that we have long held dear; it involves the subordination of civil liberties to military dictation; it imperils the freedom of individual conscience and establishes in our midst that militarism which menaces all social graces and divides the peoples of all nations. We re-affirm our determined resistance to all that is established by the Act. We cannot assist in warfare. War, which to us is wrong. War, which the peoples do not seek, will only be made impossible when men, who so believe, remain steadfast to their convictions. Conscience, it is true, has been recognised in the Act, but it has been placed at the mercy of tribunals. We are prepared to answer for our faith before any tribunal, but we cannot accept any exemption that would compel those who hate war to kill by proxy or set them to tasks which would help in the furtherance of war. We strongly condemn the monstrous assumption by parliament that a man is deemed to be bound by an oath that he has never taken and forced under an authority he will never acknowledge to perform acts which outrage his deepest convictions.

It is true that the present Act applies only to a small section of the community, but a great tradition has been sacrificed. Already there is a clamour for an extension of the Act. Admit the principle, and who can stay the march of militarism? Repeal the Act. That is your only safeguard.

If this be not done, militarism will fasten its iron grip upon our national life and institutions. There will be imposed upon us the very system which statesmen affirm that they set out to overthrow.

What shall it profit the nation if it shall win the war and lose its own soul?[37]

The eight members of the national committee, including Fenner Brockway, Barratt Brown and, of course, Morgan Jones were all found guilty and each fined £100, the maximum penalty which could be imposed. If the defendants refused to pay the fine, then each was to face 61 days imprisonment.[38]

The following month, the national committee members appealed the judgement and on this occasion Jones was brought from Cardiff prison, with an escort of two policemen, to appear with his fellow committee members. The ILP paper, *Labour Leader*, reported that there was a great deal of interest in the evidence presented by Jones and although he 'looked white and worn' he responded to the questions asked of him 'with great spirit and determination'. He explained to the court that he'd been kept in solitary confinement for three weeks but that he had "no doubt" about the stand he was taking.[39]

As expected, the appeal was rejected, the convictions were upheld and most of those convicted chose to go to prison. On leaving the court, Jones was stopped by an elderly woman who told him that she was the daughter of the 19th century English free-thinker, Richard Cobden, and that if her father were alive today he would be standing alongside him.[40]

Following the Mansion House trial and the subsequent appeal, Morgan Jones now faced an appearance before Caerphilly magistrates on May 30th. From the 'mess room' of Caerphilly police station he wrote that he was feeling 'in the best of spirits' and was 'supremely happy' that he was to face 'the tests which others had to face'. He added that he did not 'rejoice in martyrdom', but he felt that it would be unfair if others suffered while he remained 'scot free'.[41]

THE DEFENDANTS.

Those charged were :

EDWARD GRUBB, M.A., the well-known Quaker author, hon. treasurer of the N.-C.F.

A. FENNER BROCKWAY, Editor of the LABOUR LEADER, hon. secretary of the N.-C.F.

W. J. CHAMBERLAIN, newspaper traveller, and late of the Publishing Staff of the *Daily Citizen*, hon. organiser.

COUNCILLOR W. H. AYLES, organising secretary of the Bristol I.L.P.

A. BARRATT BROWN, M.A., lecturer at Woodbrooke Settlement.

J. P. F. FLETCHER, lecturer for the Peace Committee of the Society of Friends.

COUNCILLOR MORGAN JONES, a prominent I.L.P. leader in South Wales.

REV. LEYTON RICHARDS, Congregational Minister at Bowdon, Cheshire.

The trial of the eight NCF national committee members was big news: Labour Leader, May 25th, 1916.

In his comments to the *Labour Leader*, Jones said he was totally unrepentant for his stance, saying:

"If I could live it over again I should do precisely the same thing – only more intensely. The Gospel of Socialism and Internationalism has been my compass. It has kept my little bark on the straight course in the midst of the turbulent seas. I doubt not that it will lead me safely yet into the Haven of Brotherhood'. [42]

Then, obliquely referring to the tactical differences which existed between the ILP and the NCF, he said:

"Never before have I been so proud of the ILP as I have been during these last months, and my joy in being associated through the medium of the NCF, with those who do not exactly take the ILP point of view, in regard to our internal problems, has been unbounded. I shall hope to meet them again when peace has been re-established and to work with them (I trust in the ILP!) for the amelioration of the lot of the common people".[43]

After this appearance at the magistrates it seems that Morgan Jones was released and when the pacifist philosopher Bertrand Russell visited Wales in July 1916, the two met for 'lunch and a country walk'.[44] According to Russell's correspondence, he saw Jones, who he understandably thought was a Reverend, as a key figure in the pacifist movement, describing him as 'a real saint'.[45]

Jones appeared before Caerphilly magistrates again – this time charged with being an 'absentee' – where he was found guilty, fined £2 and placed in the hands of the military.[46] Jones was to remain in custody of one form or other until the end of 1917, followed by a further period in military detention in 1919, after the Great War had ended.

A Red Cross garden party to raise funds for the war wounded, Bargoed Hall, circa 1917. (Courtsey of Paul James)

Following this appearance before Caerphilly magistrates, Jones then faced a Court Martial, presumably in Cardiff. According to the *Labour Leader* he gave a 'brilliant exposition of the ILP position'.[47] The Court Martial's verdict was that he was guilty of desertion and he was sentenced to 'sheer hard labour' with the military.[48] Initially, he was sent to the Kinmel Park Army Camp near Abergele on the north Wales coast to serve his sentence, where Jones said he had nothing to complain about, apart from the food which he found 'appallingly bad'.[49] Things were to change, however, when he was transferred to Wormwood Scrubs prison.

The conditions in the 'Scrubs' were appalling and Jones was subjected to long periods of solitary confinement in a small, bare and windowless cell 'with nothing but four blank walls to look at all day long'. The only exercise he experienced was pacing 'a distance of about 10 feet, for hour after hour'. Personal abuse was also a regular occurrence and his diet consisted largely of bread and water.[50] Jones had never been a robust man and, before long, both his physical and mental health began to suffer. Indeed, Emrys Hughes, a close ILP friend of Jones, who was also a conscientious objector, was of the view that his colleague had suffered a nervous breakdown.[51]

During this period of imprisonment, Jones gave deep thought to the nature and purpose of conscientious objection and, although he had held an absolutist position up until this point, he now came to the view that the absolutist case was intellectually flawed. From the end of 1916 therefore, Jones embraced the alternativist position. This was not a decision he took lightly and he may well have equivocated a great deal before he finally committed himself.[52] He was very well aware that this change of stance would be strongly criticised by many of his closest colleagues, both within the ILP and the leadership of the NCF. Nevertheless, Morgan Jones believed that to embrace the alternativist position was morally the right thing to do and it was more likely to be effective in furthering the aims of conscientious objectors than maintaining an absolutist position.[53] Following his decision, Jones was transferred, in mid-November 1916, to the Home Office Work Centre in Warwick.[54]

His poor mental health prevented him from explaining why he had changed his position on conscription to his supporters. On November 25th, 1916, Jones wrote a 'holding letter' to the editor of the *Merthyr Pioneer* explaining why he had previously been unable to set-out his views:

'Sir – Will you allow me a little space in your columns to inform my comrades in South Wales that I have been released from prison, and that I am for the present domiciled at Warwick, where I arrived on Saturday, November 11? That means, of course, that I have deemed it wise, having regard to all the circumstances to accept alternative service, under the auspices of the Home Office Committee. I

*have not found it possible hitherto to send a considered statement of my position
owing to my complete inability to exercise sufficient mental concentration for such
a purpose – the effect, presumably, of the prison confinement. But I am happy
to say that I am quickly improving, and I trust it will shortly be possible for me
to send such a statement for publication, with your permission, in the Pioneer.
Meanwhile, I know that I may rely upon my comrades in South Wales exercising
forbearance by suspending judgement a little longer, if perchance, they disagree
with my action. In conclusion, let me thank all the comrades in the movement
who, in various ways, have given me their encouragement and have expressed
their good wishes since I was first arrested. Especially I desire to acknowledge
my indebtedness to those who have sent encouraging messages to my relatives at
home. Such thoughtfulness on the part of my comrades has, indeed, placed me
under a great obligation to them all. Perhaps they will accept these words as a
feeble expression of my gratitude.*

*Yours etc.
Morgan Jones
The Settlement, Warwick,
November 22 1916'*[55]

Morgan Jones was not, in fact, able to explain the reason for his *volte-face* for
some weeks after he had been moved to Warwick. This was the result of the
enormous strain which he was subjected to in Wormwood Scrubs and the
effect it had on him can be seen also in a letter he wrote to Catherine Marshall,
the secretary of the NCF, in mid-November.[56] He wrote to Marshall that he
was not able to discuss with her in writing the 'position' of the absolutists
and the alternativists because he was 'intellectually incapable of the effort'.
He explained that 'the effect of prison' upon his mind had been to entirely
deprive him of 'the power of mentally concentrating upon any subject for
any length of time'. He went on to say that he was 'recovering somewhat
rapidly', but that when he left the gaol it was 'quite impossible' for him to
follow any conversation or discussion for any length of time. Even though he
had been out of prison for a couple of weeks, he explained that 'even now that
disability remains with me unless I happen to be subjected to outside stimulus.
There has to be some kind of mental prodding done', he said, 'before my
mind can be stirred to activity. It is a horrible feeling I have – but there it is'.
Not only did Morgan Jones feel unable to discuss the position of alternativists
and absolutists, he also believed that he would be unable to 'even consider
anything in the nature of propaganda work this side of Christmas'.[57]

His letter concluded by stating that he would have to 'exercise forbearance'
until such time as his mind was 'rescued from its present nebulous condition'.

He added that, on occasions, he felt as though his scalp was 'about to fly off' and that he had 'a perpetual feeling of falling headlong into space'.[58]

However, the reason Jones had written to Marshall was not so much to explain his state of mind, rather it was to pass on a message to her from Clifford Allen, who he had been with in Wormwood Scrubs. Jones informed the NCF secretary that Clifford Allen expected to be leaving prison shortly and that she should make herself easily contactable.[59]

Soon after he had been transferred to Warwick, Jones had written to Clifford Allen, who was still in Wormwood Scrubs, in which he made no attempt to defend the alternativist position, simply indicating that:

'it would be pointless and profitless for me to enter a discussion of the 'Alternativist and Absolutist' business now. We will not emphasise differences. Let us rather emphasise agreements. And in one way at least we are certainly at one – to work together each in his own way to realise the Co-operative Commonwealth of the future'.[60]

The letter to Clifford Allen is also interesting for two other reasons: firstly, he explains that he is becoming more religious due to his incarceration. As he put it:

'I am becoming more infused with a religious fervour. I know not why that is so. The old bitternesses are leaving me – may have left me; they have been cast aside like old garments. More and more I am compelled to recognise and appreciate the value of individual character and the formative influence of religion thereon... the appeal it is making to me is very real and I intend to respond more and more. Perhaps I shall not be the loser thereby. None of us is so perfect that his soul would not be the better for a little mellowing'.[61]

The second reason why the letter to Allen is of interest relates to Jones' concern about his family back home in Wales. From his room at Warwick, he explained that one of his brothers had received his call-up papers and his brother's wife was certain (according to their doctor) that her husband would 'fail to survive' the war.[62] Jones feared the effect that his brother being called-up would have on his 'poor mother' and, in fact, he was worried that this 'may well prove too much for her'. Another of Jones' brothers, who was also a conscientious objector, had been obliged to give up his teaching post, because of his anti-war views, and he was now a labourer. Then, to crown his concerns, Jones stated that his own matrimonial engagement was in 'serious jeopardy'.[63] His fears were justified, and the engagement did not last.

If Jones was not able to explain his support for the alternativist position when he was first moved to Warwick, he set out his case in some detail in

Morgan Jones prior to the imprisonment which took such a toll on his health.

early 1917. As one would expect, he chose the letters section of the ILP's *Merthyr Pioneer* to do so and he set out his case in direct response to his critics.[64]

When Morgan Jones' decision to embrace the alternativist view became known, he was immediately subjected to a torrent of criticism from absolutists. The national leaders of the NCF were, as he expected, extremely critical, but so were a number of the local activists in Wales who he had campaigned with. In fact, they were so incensed that some of them wrote an anonymous letter to the *Merthyr Pioneer* hinting strongly that Morgan Jones was guilty of cowardice.[65]

This obviously caused him great hurt and, as soon as he was able, he wrote a long two-part letter to the *Pioneer* setting-out in great detail the reasons why he now held the alternativist position. His writing is somewhat convoluted, no doubt due to the continuing effect of how he was treated in prison, but two arguments are set out with some force.[66]

Firstly, Jones argued that in his view 'opposition to the state' should be confined to opposition to 'militarism' and not taken further. Morgan argued that the struggle against conscription was essentially a moral issue and rested on personal conscience. Although he 'hated the Government', he maintained that his opposition to warfare 'was occasioned by deep moral convictions' and not by hostility inspired by wider political objectives.[67]

Perhaps more significantly, Morgan Jones also pointed out, with some justification, that the difference between alternativists and absolutists was, in practice, not as great as often assumed. There were, he argued, two kinds of absolutists – those who were granted 'exemption certificates' by a tribunal and as a consequence were instructed to carry out work of national importance. Such men, he said, were in reality alternativists, even if they did not see themselves in this way. The second category of absolutists were those, like himself initially, who went to prison and undertook prison work, such as gardening, making ships' fenders or sewing mailbags. The situation was clear cut when the COs were in military camps, but once prisoners were transferred to civil prisons 'the whole pitch was queered for the absolutists immediately'. In his argument, Jones referred to mailbags. In prisons these were being made by absolutists and were then being used by the army to convey messages to the frontline and those messages might lead to 'the sacrifice of thousands of lives'. Jones accepted that some might think that this example 'might be stretching the point', but he believed that COs had to have a logically defensible position; either they were to refuse virtually all forms of work or they ought to recognise the reality of their positions and admit that they were not really absolutists at all.[68]

A well-argued response to Jones' assertion came from Mansel Grenfell, the brother of the future MP for Gower and an absolutist CO.[69] Grenfell had also been in prison in Wormwood Scrubs before being transferred to the Kinmel Park Army Camp, and wrote a long letter to the *Merthyr Pioneer*. In a comradely way, he did not really contradict Jones' assertions about the blurring of the dividing lines between the two types of COs but, from a socialist standpoint, Grenfell suggested his colleague was wrong to criticise absolutists. While he indicated that he appreciated the pressure Jones had been under, he argued that those COs holding one point of view ought not to criticise other COs who held a different view.[70]

If some activists were, to varying degrees, critical of Jones, others were more supportive. Significantly, soon after Jones made it known that he was embracing alternativism, he was re-elected to the NCF national committee.[71] Support also came from somewhat unexpected quarters. Walter Newbold, a CO ILPer who later became the Communist Party's first MP, wrote to the *Merthyr Pioneer* to express his 'pleasure' at Morgan Jones' statement on alternativism. He indicated that he was also a CO who had initially been an absolutist, but was now convinced that alternativism was the way forward.[72]

One of those most critical of Jones on the NCF executive, and who strongly adhered to the absolutist position, was its chairman, Clifford Allen. In February 1918 he claimed that Morgan Jones had 'no interest left' in the conscientious objection movement and had instead become 'engrossed' in securing a parliamentary candidature.

Jones' other principal adversary on the NCF executive was Fenner Brockway, the founder of the NCF. Like Allen, Brockway believed that the COs should not compromise with the state and the absolutist case was strongly expressed in the pages of the NCF's journal, *The Tribunal*.[74]

Many years later, Fenner Brockway expressed the view to Morgan Jones' son-in-law that Jones' decision to become an alternativist was in line with his inherent inclination to be pragmatic and to seek compromise.[75] This astute assessment places Morgan Jones' decision in a wider context, as Fenner

Brockway clearly saw Jones' change in position as being consistent with his longer term approach to politics.

Not only were there differences over alternativism between Morgan Jones and the NCF leadership, there were also disagreements over the NCF leadership's support for workers' soviets, or councils, after the Russian Revolution. Jones took the view that the NCF should confine itself to opposing conscription and upholding the right to conscience.[76]

However, when examining Morgan Jones' decision to become an alternativist, it is impossible to see it as being divorced from the physical and mental privation he was suffering. Having read his letters to the *Merthyr Pioneer*, it is difficult not to conclude that his decision was in part, at least regarding its timing, related to his state of mental health.

After his transfer to Warwick, Jones' physical health continued to deteriorate, which led to him being released at the end of 1917,[77] but this did not mean the end of his agitational work. Quite the opposite. Despite being shouted down at public meetings and continuously followed by plain clothes police officers, he travelled all over south Wales spreading the anti-war message.[78]

Even though the Great War had ended in November 1918, conscription continued until 1920 and Britain also became involved in military action in Russia, supporting the White Army against the Bolsheviks. As a consequence Morgan Jones' opposition to conscription and his advocacy of peace did not wane. It was therefore no surprise that he again found himself before Bargoed magistrates, in April 1919, some five months after the First World War had ended.[79]

Bizarrely, on this occasion he was charged with deserting from the Lancashire Fusiliers.[80] No representative of the army was present at the hearing and, despite his evident ill health, Morgan Jones spoke forcefully in his own defence. He stated that he had never been in the Regiment it was claimed he had deserted from, and that for three years he had been "pursued and persecuted" for his beliefs. The real reason for his arrest, said Jones, was his continuing involvement in anti-war campaigning.[81] After the magistrate had adjourned the case on two occasions, a lieutenant of the Lancashire Fusiliers gave evidence that the military authorities had received "instructions" that Jones was to be arrested and should be handed over.[82] Earlier, a local police sergeant had given evidence that Jones had compèred and spoken at an ILP-organised concert in Bargoed at which Eduard Soermus, a Russian violinist who was touring Wales, had played music which, it was alleged, inspired the Russian Revolution.[83] During the concert, the violinist had decided to speak out in support of the revolution and, according to the police officer, Morgan Jones had paid tribute to the German revolutionaries Karl Liebknecht and Rosa Luxembourg, both of whom had been recently murdered by the *Freikorps* militia in Berlin.

The local magistrates quickly agreed that Jones should once again be placed in the hands of the military and he was duly escorted by soldiers to the Lancashire Fusiliers' camp in Bury, Lancashire.[84] Jones was kept in detention for three months, later being moved to the Blackdown Camp in Farnborough, before being abruptly released on August 2nd, 1919.[85]

The feelings of ILP activists were well summed-up by Emrys Hughes in a letter to the *Merthyr Pioneer*, which accurately summarised what had happened to Morgan Jones: 'six months after the conclusion of hostilities, six months after the end of the war to crush militarism, one of the most prominent public men in south Wales, a member of a District Council, one whose sincerity and good faith is recognised right throughout the district, has been brought to a Police Court, refused a hearing, found guilty of a crime of which he is innocent, and sent away to a regiment he never belonged to'.[86]

Release from the army camp was not, however, the end of the story. On Gelligaer UDC there was an unsuccessful attempt to remove Jones from the local War Pensions committee[87] and, more seriously, when Morgan Jones returned to Wales he found himself prevented from returning to his job as school teacher. Even though representations were made by Gelligaer Trades and Labour Council, the Education Committee of Glamorgan County Council 'absolutely refused to re-open the question'.[88] Despite his poor health, Morgan Jones had no alternative but to find work underground in a local colliery.

Fortunately, within a few months, Jones secured the salaried post of the ILP's Welsh organiser and he became a member of the National Council of the ILP.[89] Although already an elected member of Gelligaer UDC, in March 1919 he also stood for election to the Glamorgan County Council. Described in one local newspaper as 'the most unpopular man in the locality', he contested the Bargoed ward.[90] At the time, Morgan Phillips, who had been taught in school by Morgan Jones and later became general secretary of the Labour Party, was a local ILP member. In his recently published autobiography he referred to the local election campaign and, although Morgan Phillips got the year of the election wrong, he recalled how, 'Morgan Jones was bitterly attacked by ex-servicemen's organisations because of his pacifist activities and propaganda during the war. Our meetings were broken up, stones were thrown and the windows of the ILP rooms shattered'.[91] As expected, Morgan Jones' election campaign was unsuccessful.[92]

However, in December 1919, Jones had another opportunity when county councillor, Reverend D. Leyshon Evans, a Congregational Minister, died suddenly.[93] This time Morgan Jones was elected, although no record of the actual result exists. Yet, despite his victory, feelings about Jones' opposition to the war were still very strong. This was made very apparent when he attended his first council meeting. Breaking with convention, no welcome or congratulations were offered to him on his election either by the chairman of the council or by any of his fellow councillors.[94]

Morgan Jones had made a principled stand against the war and against conscription. His opposition had been widely condemned, not least in his own community, and as the war dragged on, and the casualty list grew longer, so the hostility to Jones became more intense. It is perhaps difficult for us today to imagine the enormous strain taking such a stance must have placed on Jones and his family. Opposing the First World War needed huge courage and commitment. Morgan Jones had both.

As the years passed, many of those who had deprecated Jones' stance increasingly came to respect both the man and his principles. The cost however to his health was very high. He was never a robust man and the harsh treatment which he suffered while imprisoned was almost certainly one of the reasons why he was to die at a relatively early age.

Notes

1. For Morgan Jones' views on the First World War see the *Merthyr Express*, April 1st, 1916 and the *Merthyr Pioneer* April 1st, 1916.
2. *Merthyr Pioneer*, January 24th, 1916.
3. Dylan Rees, *Dictionary of Labour Biography*, op. cit., p.146.
4. Information from Alun Burge.
5. *Merthyr Express*, November 17th, 1914. See 'Bargoed and Gilfach – A Local History' for details of the recruitment process, Gelligaer Historical Society, 2011.
6. *Merthyr Express*, November 17th, 1914.
7. *Caerphilly Journal*, November 17th, 1914.
8. Ibid.
9. *Caerphilly Journal*, November 24th, 1914.
10. See the *Caerphilly Journal* throughout the autumn of 1914.
11. *Caerphilly Journal*, December 1st, 1914.
12. *Caerphilly Journal*, October 5th, 1914.
13. *Caerphilly Journal*, September 24th, 1914. For further examples of support for the war see Kay David, *The Rhymney Valley and the Great War: 1914-18*, (Lewis Boys Comprehensive School, 1992).
14. *Caerphilly Journal*, October 30th, 1914.
15. In fact, there is no reference to Morgan Jones' views on the war in any newspaper in 1914 and 1915.
16. Both the *Merthyr Express* and the *Caerphilly Journal* carried almost weekly reports and photographs, throughout 1915 and 1916, of local young men who had lost their lives in the First World War.
17. *Caerphilly Journal*, October 29th, 1915.
18. *Merthyr Pioneer*, February 19th, 1916.
19. *Merthyr Pioneer*, January 29th, 1916.
20. Ibid.

21. Dylan Rees, *Dictionary of Labour Biography*, op. cit., p.146.
22. Minutes of Gelligaer UDC, op. cit., Glamorgan Archives, UDG/C/1/11.
23. Ibid.
24. Ibid.
25. *Merthyr Express*, April 1st, 1916, and *Merthyr Pioneer*, April 1st, 1916.
26. Ibid.
27. Ibid.
28. Ibid.
29. Ibid.
30. Ibid.
31. Letter re-printed in *Llafur* (Journal for the Study of Welsh Labour History), Vol. 1, No. 4, 1975.
32. Ibid.
33. *Merthyr Pioneer*, August 3rd, 1916.
34. Ibid.
35. *Caerphilly Journal*, June 8th, 1916.
36. *Labour Leader*, May 18th, 1916.
37. Ibid.
38. *Labour Leader*, May 25th, 1916.
39. *Labour Leader*, August 3rd, 1916.
40. Ibid.
41. *Caerphilly Journal*, June 8th, 1916.
42. *Labour Leader*, June 1st, 1916.
43. Ibid.
44. Letter from Bertrand Russell, June 1916, reprinted in *The Autobiography of Bertrand Russell*, (Routledge, 2000), p.293.
45. Ibid.
46. *Caerphilly Journal*, June 22nd, 1916.
47. *Labour Leader*, June 29th, 1916.
48. Ibid.
49. Brock Millman, *Managing Dissent in First World War Britain*, (Frank Cass, 2014), p.203.
50. *Merthyr Pioneer*, July 21st, 1916.
51. Ibid.
52. Aled Eirug, *The Opposition to the Great War in Wales 1914-1918*, (University of Wales Press, 2018), pp.203-4.
53. Morgan Jones' arguments are set out in a number of letters he wrote to the *Merthyr Pioneer* in early 1917.
54. This can be deduced from the correspondence from Morgan Jones reproduced in *Llafur*, op. cit.
55. *Merthyr Pioneer*, November 30th, 1916.
56. Letter to C. Marshall from Morgan Jones reproduced in *Llafur*, op. cit.
57. Ibid.
58. Ibid.
59. Ibid.
60. Letter to C. Allen reproduced in *Llafur*, op. cit.
61. Ibid.
62. Ibid.
63. Ibid.

64. *Merthyr Pioneer*, February 3rd and February 10th, 1917.
65. *Merthyr Pioneer*, October 21st, 1916.
66. *Merthyr Pioneer*, op. cit.
67. *Merthyr Pioneer*, February 3rd, 1917.
68. *Merthyr Pioneer*, February 10th, 1917.
69. *Merthyr Pioneer*, February 24th and March 24th, 1917.
70. *Merthyr Pioneer*, March 24th, 1917.
71. Aled Eirug, unpublished PhD. thesis (2017). Morgan Jones was successful in the contest for the Welsh seat on the executive against Emyrs Hughes.
72. *Merthyr Pioneer*, March 3rd, 1917.
73. Martin Gilbert, *Plough My Own Furrow - The Story of Lord Allen of Hurtwood as told through his Writings and Correspondence*, (Longmans, 1965), p.109.
74. I am appreciative of Aled Eirug for sight of copies of the NCF's *The Tribunal* which clearly set out the NCF leadership's view.
75. Conversation with John and Margaret Sheaff, summer 2015.
76. Aled Eirug. op. cit., p.157.
77. *Merthyr Pioneer*, November 17th, 1917.
78. See, for example, *Merthyr Pioneer*, August 10th, 1918 and March 1st, 1919.
79. *Merthyr Pioneer*, May 17th, 1919.
80. Ibid.
81. Ibid.
82. Ibid.
83. See Colin Thomas' article on the 'Red Violinist' in the *Western Mail*, July 29th, 2017.
84. *Merthyr Pioneer*, August 9th, 1919.
85. *The Tribunal*, July 27th, 1919.
86. *Merthyr Pioneer*, May 17th, 1919.
87. Ibid.
88. Ibid.
89. Dylan Rees, *Dictionary of Labour Biography*, op. cit., p.146.
90. *Merthyr Express*, March 18th, 1919.
91. Morgan Phillips, *Morgan Phillips: Labour Party Secretary; Socialist International Chairman*, Ed. Morgan D. Phillips, (Spokesman Books, 2017), p.22.
92. *Merthyr Express*, April 8th, 1919.
93. *Merthyr Express*, December 16th, 1919.
94. *Merthyr Express*, January 13th, 1920.

3

The Caerphilly By-election of 1921

Since the formation of the Caerphilly parliamentary division in 1918, its Member of Parliament had been the Labour Party's Alfred Onions. Originally from Staffordshire, Onions had moved to Risca as a young man and found work in the local collieries. He was appointed a miners' checkweigher – a vitally important post at a time when miners' wages were determined by the weight of the coal they mined – became secretary of the Monmouthshire miners, went on to be the miners' agent for the Sirhowy Valley, and was elected treasurer of the South Wales Miners' Federation (SWMF). He also represented south Wales on the Miners' Federation of Great Britain (MFGB) executive. In terms of his approach to industrial relations, Alfred Onions was very much a moderate, believing that conciliation and round table discussions in the coal industry were far preferable to industrial conflict. As such, Onions was part of a diminishing group of Federation leaders who were being increasingly challenged by a more radical generation: men who believed in the effectiveness of class conflict, and had as their objectives socialism and workers' control.[1]

In public life, outside of the coal industry, Alfred Onions had also been very active. He had been a founder member of Risca UDC, its first chairman, and for 20 years he had served on Monmouthshire County Council, becoming an alderman and its chairman in 1918. Alfred Onions was also a magistrate.[2]

Given these commitments, it was hardly surprising that he seldom spoke in, or even attended, the House of Commons.[3] The Federation leadership tended to see the securing of a parliamentary seat in a mining area as a reward for loyal and long service to the union, and like a number of his generation of Federation leaders, Alfred Onions placed far more importance on industrial and local leadership than on parliamentary representation. For him, parliament was a useful platform to be used from time to time, rather than an instrument for radical social change.

In common with most of the SWMF leadership, Onions had been a strong supporter of Britain's involvement in the Great War and his four children, including his daughter, all saw active service. His eldest son, a lieutenant in the Third Battalion Monmouth Regiment, was killed in France and the heartbreak this caused Onions almost certainly contributed to a 'long illness' which eventually led to his death in July 1921.[4]

Because of his ill health, Onions had let it be known in early 1921 that he would not be seeking re-election as Labour candidate for the next election and the miners had begun the process of selecting another candidate months before his death. The favourite for the nomination had been Alderman Albert Thomas J.P., the miners' agent and secretary of the Rhymney Valley District of the SWMF and, when Onions died, he was seen as the most likely candidate to fight the by-election. After he suddenly withdrew, another name mentioned was that of Frank Hodges, the moderate secretary of the MFGB, who had been the miners' agent for the Garw Valley.[5] As it turned out, Frank Hodges' popularity plummeted after the 1921 miners' lock-out and he too did not allow his name to go forward. Eventually, after a single transferable vote ballot, it was William Harris of Pontllanfraith who emerged as the miners' nominee.[6]

William Harris had been the political organiser for the miners in Monmouthshire for the previous ten years, and his background and political and industrial views were very similar to those of Alfred Onions. In other words, he was very much part of the Federation establishment. Like Onions, Harris had been a checkweigher and had worked his way up the Federation ranks to become a member of the SWMF executive. He also had a background in local government, having been a councillor for eight years on Abertillery UDC. His political experience included being election agent to a clutch of south Wales miners' MPs, including William Brace, the very influential President of the SWMF. William Harris was a strong Baptist and having backed the war effort he made it known that he had the support of ex-servicemen.[7]

Although it had been rumoured that Ramsay MacDonald and Philip Snowden might be interested in contesting the seat, the only non-mining person who allowed his name to go forward for the Labour nomination turned out to be Morgan Jones.[8] With the support of the ILP, Jones won the backing of the Co-operative Movement and the National Union of Railwaymen; the nominations he received from the miners' lodges were declared inadmissible because he was not a member of the Federation.[9]

A ballot to select the by-election candidate, from amongst members of the organisations affiliated to the Labour Party in the constituency, was held on August 3rd and 4th. The result was expected to be close but to many people's surprise, Morgan Jones secured the nomination with 7,303 votes, compared to 3,108 for William Harris. With many rank-and-file miners having cast their vote for Jones, he was duly selected as the Labour candidate.[10]

The vote for the nomination spoke volumes about how the Labour movement in the Rhymney Valley was changing politically. Not only was this a vote in favour of the local and more youthful candidate – Morgan Jones was 36, whereas William Harris was 53 – at a time when being an MP tended to be seen as an older man's profession, it was a deliberate vote in favour of a socialist and an anti-war candidate. Indeed, it was a decisive vote for a prominent conscientious objector to be the Labour candidate. Jones, on being told of his success, began to set the tone of the forthcoming by-election by saying that he was a native of the constituency and understood the social and political life of the community.[11]

Some weeks later, in a newspaper article, Morgan Jones recalled the selection conference and the emotional scenes which greeted his selection:

"Women, and even men shed tears … tears of joy that at last the persecutors were to be fought by the persecuted. And I remember with what a fierce shout they re-echoed my declaration that the election was to be fought not as a purely defensive effort, but rather as a general frontal attack upon capitalism's strongest entrenchments. That meeting will live in my memory".[12]

Some two years after the Armistice, for many miners the war was not the divisive issue it had been previously. No doubt, even those who had disagreed with the pacifist position had respect for the conscientious objectors who had stood by their principles. There was also a growing feeling that the Great War had not been worth the terrible human sacrifice.

Crucially, though, there was now a real sense of growing militancy among the miners, just as the halcyon days of the south Wales coalfield were clearly coming to an end. Internationally, the supremacy of Welsh coal was being challenged and, against the back-drop of economic recession, the coal owners were once again in charge of the industry after the government had relinquished their war-time control. The coal owners quickly gave notice of their intention to introduce wage cuts and redundancies, while unemployment was rising and, as a consequence, there was now real hardship in mining communities. In response to the wage reductions proposed by the coal owners, the miners, railwaymen and transport workers came together and formed the Triple Alliance, but this came to an ignominious end on April 15th, 1921 when, on 'Black Friday', the miners were left high and dry by their Labour movement colleagues.

As a result of this 'betrayal' there was huge anger among the miners, which erupted in Caerphilly the following weekend when an angry crowd of between 500 and 600 gathered and attacked the police station – where a local miner was being held – with rocks and stones. Police reinforcements were brought in from the surrounding villages and about 50 officers from the Sussex and Essex constabularies were drafted in to maintain order.[13]

After Black Friday, there followed a three-month lock-out which ended in the miners returning to work having been totally defeated. This led to an unprecedented mood of anger and bitterness across the entire British coalfield, not least in south Wales and the Rhymney Valley, where the miners were now facing huge wage cuts. This was the essential backdrop to the Caerphilly by-election.

Given that the miners in the Caerphilly constituency were becoming increasingly militant, and there was a growing restlessness across Britain, it is hardly surprising that the newly-formed Communist Party of Great Britain (CPGB) took the opportunity to field a parliamentary candidate for the first time.[14] The CPGB took its inspiration and method of organisation from the Russian Bolsheviks, and their revolution of 1917, and elements of the British establishment feared a similar attempt at revolution happening in Britain.

Because of the rising discontent in industrial Wales, the CPGB saw the coalfield as one of its most fertile recruiting grounds. An eclectic range of left wingers, including syndicalists – who believed in workers' control and the centrality of trade union organisation – had been quickly drawn to the new revolutionary party. The SWMF was also one of the main supporters of the Marxist Central Labour College, where the brightest activists were being sent for independent working class education.[15] The CPGB had been delighted too that a SWMF delegate conference had recently agreed to affiliate to the Communist Third International, but were equally incensed that the Labour Party's national conference had decided to prevent the Communist Party affiliating to the Labour Party.

In the highly charged atmosphere of the south Wales coalfield, the Communist Party saw the Caerphilly by-election as a real opportunity to raise its profile and build its support, at the expense of the Labour Party. Moreover, Caerphilly was fertile ground for the Communist Party.[16] There was, according to a local newspaper columnist, 'not a division in England and Wales in which they have a greater professed following'.[17]

The CPGB candidate in the by-election was Bob Stewart, a fiery Scotsman who had been imprisoned for his activities during the recent miners' lock-out. In line with the CPGB's vanguardist structure, he was appointed as candidate by the CPGB's central committee.[18]

In the general election of 1918, the only challenge to Alfred Onions had come from the Liberal Party candidate, William Rees Edmunds, a solicitor from Merthyr Tydfil, who had received a very respectable 9,482 votes compared with 11,496 for the Labour Party candidate. As the by-election approached, the Liberal Association quickly confirmed that Rees Edmunds would be standing again.[19] In 1918, there had been no Conservative and Unionist candidate, and the local Conservative Association, after some equivocation, now decided that they would throw their weight behind Rees Edmunds, especially as he was going to stand as a Coalition-Liberal candidate in support of the Lloyd George Liberal-Conservative Coalition Government.[20] The decision was warmly welcomed by local Tory supporters because, when it was learnt that Morgan Jones was to be the Labour candidate, they felt that the chance of contributing to the defeat of a Labour 'conshie' was far more important than fighting for a respectable Tory vote.[21]

With the candidates duly selected, there followed a short, sharp election contest lasting a mere eight days, leading up to the election on August 24th. In 1921, the Caerphilly parliamentary division extended from the very top of the Rhymney Valley and included virtually the whole of the Glamorgan side of the valley down to and including Caerphilly town, westwards to take in Nelson, Treharris, Trelewis and Bedlinog, and further south to include Taff's Well. Since 1918, the electorate had increased by 15,000 to 34,512, of which only about 14,000 were women because of the limited female franchise.[22]

The election campaigns of the three candidates encompassed all parts of the division and beyond, with public meetings attracting hundreds, even thousands as the election reached its climax. Prominent Labour figures including Ramsay MacDonald and Arthur Henderson MP came to the division to speak at public meetings and the Liberals and Conservatives similarly provided a host of MPs, and Lloyd George, the prime minister, sent no fewer than three messages of support to the Coalition candidate. The Communist Party also attracted a huge amount of attention because of their highly energetic campaign.[23]

The contest had all the ingredients for an exciting election and it provided plenty of column inches for the papers,

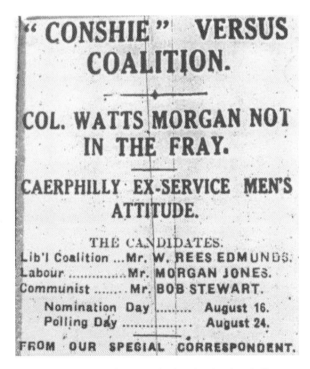

"CONSHIE" VERSUS COALITION.

COL. WATTS MORGAN NOT IN THE FRAY.

CAERPHILLY EX-SERVICE MEN'S ATTITUDE.

THE CANDIDATES:
Lib'l Coalition ...Mr. W. REES EDMUNDS.
Labour ....Mr. MORGAN JONES.
Communist ....Mr. BOB STEWART.

Nomination Day .... August 16.
Polling Day .... August 24.

FROM OUR SPECIAL CORRESPONDENT.

'Conshie versus Coalition' - the by-election battle lines are drawn: Western Mail, August 15th, 1921.

both inside Wales and beyond. The coverage of the election was not, of course, objective in any way with virtually all the newspapers who covered the election displaying varying degrees of anti-Labour bias but it was the *Western Mail*, the traditional paper of the coal owners, which led the way as the most vitriolic of the anti-Labour newspapers.[24]

The opening salvo in the campaign came from the Communist Party. Despite press suggestions that if Morgan Jones was selected as the Labour candidate the CP may not field a candidate, the Communists made it clear before Labour had selected Jones that they intended to contest the seat. Bob Stewart, who was still in prison and would be there for most of the campaign, declared that they had 'an abundance of damaging ammunition' ready to be fired at the Labour Party and the ILP.[25] They were out, it was said, to 'fight the Labour Party, and especially the ILP'.[26] As the CP stated in one of its own publications, they intended to contest Caerphilly 'to demonstrate just how far and what way revolutionary political action differs from the creeping thing the worker has learned to know and hate as parliamentarianism'.[27]

The Communist Party put a huge effort into this, their first parliamentary election. Two supplements of the weekly *Communist* were devoted to the campaign and then, in addition to the election address, further leaflets were produced. Small wonder the Labour Party described the Communists' campaign as 'lavish',[28] and although the fledgling party lacked a strong local structure, 'militants' came to help from all across the south Wales valleys and further afield.[29] To the delight of the CP, the Labour Party ward in the village of Bedlinog defected *en bloc* to their cause. Yet, despite the CP generating a lot of political capital out of this, it was a one-off.[30] Under the leadership of the activist, Edgar Evans – 'Edgar the Ironmonger' as he was known locally – the defections meant that the Labour Party in Bedlinog was left without a functioning campaign committee.[31]

The Communists' main slogan during the election was 'All Power to the Workers',[32] and their determination to demonstrate their growing strength was shown by the fact that they brought in nearly all their best known speakers – Willie Gallagher, Harry Pollitt, Helen Crawford, William Paul, Joe Vaughan, Walton Newbold, Arthur MacMannus and Tommy Jackson.[33] This impressive roll call was even supplemented by a visit by John McLean, the celebrated Scottish revolutionary.[34] Jack Jones, the future Welsh novelist and playwright, who was a member of the CP at the time, commented in his autobiography that 'every available Communist speaker in Britain invaded the division',[35] even though they had some difficulty with the Welsh place-names. He also describes how party officials from London were brought in to organise the campaign and there were even 'a couple of observers from abroad'.[36]

Jack Jones himself was given a key role in the campaign, organising Communist speakers for the many meetings. Jones even introduced the candidate, Bob Stewart, at his first meeting – at the Twyn in the centre of Caerphilly – just after he had been released from Cardiff prison.[37]

In his autobiography, Bob Stewart wrote at some length about his experience of the by-election. Rather disparagingly, he thought Morgan Jones was 'a nice chap but not a virile working-class politician',[38] and he referred to Tommy Jackson dismissing Jones' religious non-conformity by saying 'this endeared him to the old women of both sexes':[39] a comment which probably said more about the Communist Party than it did about Morgan Jones and the Labour Party.

It was perhaps a sign of the CP's wishful thinking that, on one occasion, Tommy Jackson was addressing a public meeting in Caerphilly when he noticed that one of the towers of Caerphilly Castle was leaning to one side. "There you are" he said, "even the castle tower is leaning to the left".[40]

If the Communist Party started their campaign early,[41] so did the coalition. Building on the electoral organisation which already existed, Rees Edmunds was quick to establish his election committee and they held their first meeting before Labour had even selected its candidate,[42] but once Morgan Jones was in place, Rees Edmunds set out two of the main themes of his election campaign. The first was the need, as he saw it, for 'unity' behind Lloyd George, 'our great countryman', in the difficult tasks facing the government, including bringing peace to Ireland and tackling unemployment. The other theme was Morgan Jones' socialism. It was clear, said Rees Edmunds, that it was 'the younger generation of the working community' who had supported Jones for the Labour nomination. Rees Edmunds believed that he was as much a Labour man as Morgan Jones but the difference was that, unlike Jones, he was not 'an exponent of a socialist regime'. Going on, Rees Edmunds stated that there was little difference between communism and socialism: both the other candidates wanted to end capitalism and the only difference was that Bob Stewart wanted 'revolution' and Morgan Jones wanted 'evolution'.[43] This was a theme which the *Western Mail*, in particular, returned to time and again during the course of the election. As an editorial of the paper commented on August 17th, 'there is no essential difference between the aim of the Labour and Communist candidates: they set their eyes towards the same goal, they differ only as to means and procedure'.[44]

The other part of the coalition message was to point out that, like Stewart, Morgan Jones had been a 'conshie'. The coalition constantly reminded people of Jones' pacifism, convinced that 'the majority of patriotic Welsh miners and their wives' would think that such a person would be 'unfit' to represent them in parliament.[45] This constant reminding was reinforced by a number of letters to the press by ex-servicemen who accused Jones of 'insulting the memory' of the war dead.[46]

Morgan Jones' campaign was also well organised. His agent was T.I. Mardy Jones, the Miners' Federation organiser from Pontypridd, assisted by T.C. Morris, Labour's Welsh organiser. ILP MPs and activists, like Dick Wallhead, the son of the future MP for Merthyr, came from all parts of south Wales and Mrs Elizabeth Andrews of the Rhondda played a key role in securing the women's vote.[47]

Contrary to some expectations, Jones' campaign team included those in the Labour movement who had supported the war as well as those who had opposed it. The presence of Brigadier-General Thompson and Lieutenant Colonel D. Watts Morgan CBE, DSO, MP, of the Miners' Federation executive and a prominent county councillor, on a number of platforms with Jones was clear evidence of the breadth of support for him. Even his agent, T.I. Mardy Jones, had been active in support of the war effort.[48] The Labour campaign also pulled together those who would have described themselves as socialists and those who did not; alongside an array of ILP MPs and major figures there were also Federation leaders drawn from the 'old guard'. Importantly, throughout the campaign, while always proclaiming his belief in socialism, Morgan Jones was at pains to project himself as a moderate and responsible Labour leader, someone who would have no truck with extremism.[49]

In his campaign speeches, Jones, not surprisingly, criticised the Coalition Government rather than going into the detail of Labour's alternatives.[50] He realised that this was, after all, a by-election at a time when working class people were experiencing real hardships, not that long after Lloyd George had won an overwhelming election victory in the so-called 'Coupon Election' of 1918.

Astutely, Jones also sought to neuter the anti-war criticism by championing the cause of ex-servicemen and their pension entitlements. In his election address, he had referred to 'the infamous treachery'[51] of the government in the way they had failed to give proper support to ex-servicemen. With unemployment increasing, Britain was clearly not the land fit for heroes which Lloyd George had promised.

In response, the coalition campaign went to great lengths to counter Jones' assertions. Ian Macpherson MP, the pensions minister, came to Caerphilly to address public meetings and even met a group of ex-servicemen who had grievances.[52] At the same time, the *Western Mail* went into overdrive on the issue, printing the fine detail of what measures the government had taken.[53] The coalition was not helped, though, when a number of unemployed miners constantly heckled and interrupted a speaker from Manchester, representing the Joint Council of Ex-Servicemen, who was speaking in support of Rees

Morgan Jones campaigning on election day. (Courtesy of the Western Mail)

Edmunds at a meeting in Deri. His attempts to blame 'local administrations' for the plight of ex-service men did not go down well.[54]

A couple of days later, when the same speaker from Manchester addressed a large, open-air meeting in Bargoed, there were similarly boisterous scenes, only this time violence broke out and a Liberal supporter was allegedly struck by a Labour supporter.[55] Indeed, as the election campaign progressed, so tempers became increasingly frayed. At Pengam, there was what the *Merthyr Express* called 'a sensational incident',[56] when Communist Party members turned-up, in a car, to a Labour open-air meeting flying a red flag and, on arrival, they began holding an alternative meeting next to the Labour one. Tempers soon flared when an ex-serviceman kicked the chair from under one of the Communist speakers. In retaliation, a Communist then delivered 'a vigorous blow'[57] to the ex-servicemen's head, apparently rendering him unconscious. As the Communist was making his retreat, 'like a hare fleeing from hounds', he was 'roughly handled' by the crowd. When the Communists left, in their car and went to a different venue, they were followed by other ex-servicemen who, this time, grabbed their red flag, threw it to the ground and stamped on it.[58]

Communists were also involved in other clashes, sometimes with Coalitionists as well as Labour supporters, such as in an open-air meeting in

Bargoed when a 'free fight'[59] occurred after Communists were late leaving a venue which had been booked by the Coalitionists. However, the most reported incident involved the Labour agent, T.I. Mardy Jones. At a meeting in Trelewis, Mardy Jones was reported to have turned-up at a Coalition meeting with four supporters and rushed to the front of the meeting. When asked by the Coalition speaker if he had come to interrupt him, it was alleged that Mardy Jones had responded by saying it was 'a lie'. He then apparently proceeded to take off his coat and challenged the Coalition speaker to a fight. The challenge was declined. The meeting nevertheless ended in uproar with Mardy Jones and his colleagues being roundly booed.[60]

As the election campaign entered its last couple of days, the Mardy Jones incident had become one of the main talking points but most attention focused on the final messages of the Coalition and Labour Party candidates. By this time it was clear that the Communists were likely to come third (bottom) in the poll. In his eve-of-poll message, Rees Edmunds drew no distinction between Labour and the Communists, stating that the real choice for the electorate was between 'constitutional progress' and the alternative of 'revolution'. Morgan Jones was labelled a 'strife maker', whereas the Coalition stood for 'peace at home and abroad'.[61]

Jones used the last part of his campaign to reiterate the messages he had previously set out: the need to tackle what he called the 'terror of unemployment', and the lack of support for ex-servicemen. A key message was also sent out regarding the Communist Party. As *The Times* accurately reported, the main aim of the Communists in the campaign was to 'queer the pitch' of the Labour candidate, and Labour certainly recognised that the Communist Party standing in the election introduced a new electoral dynamic. The concern in the Labour camp was that the Communist Party, even if it came third, might pull sufficient votes from Labour to enable the Coalition to win. The Labour campaign therefore made a number of direct appeals to its voters to remain loyal and not be beguiled by 'the rhetoric of revolution'.[62]

After eight days of frenetic campaigning, the election count was held immediately after the polls had closed, at the Twyn council offices in Caerphilly town centre. A large crowd assembled outside and, to keep themselves entertained, party supporters sang a variety of Welsh hymns and popular songs. There was an immediate silence, however, when the returning officer appeared at an upstairs window of the council offices, but the silence was short lived because when the first candidate's vote – the vote for Morgan Jones – was announced the crowd erupted into 'tumultuous cheering', which continued for the rest of the declaration.[63]

Labour supporters gather outside the ILP offices in Bargoed after Morgan Jones' victory.
(Courtesy of the Rhymney Valley Express)

The result of the 1921 Caerphilly by-election was:

Morgan Jones	Labour	13,699
W.R. Edmunds	National Liberal	8,958
R. Stewart	Communist	2,592
Majority		4,741

When Jones appeared at the window, there was further cheering and after he gave his thanks to his supporters they carried him shoulder high to the Labour committee rooms.[64]

Arthur Henderson, Labour's chief whip in the House of Commons, immediately sent Jones a telegram to congratulate him on his 'magnificent victory for Labour', adding that he had 'not only successfully resisted the combined attacks of the representatives of capitalist domination and communist dictatorship', he had also 'greatly strengthened' the position of the Labour Party.[65]

True to form, the *Western Mail* carried spurious complaints from the unsuccessful campaigns alleging breaches of electoral rules but, as expected, there was no substance behind these complaints.[66] *The Times,* to its credit, accurately stated that the result was 'a sweeping triumph for the Labour candidate'.[67] Not only did the Labour vote increase substantially, but the coalition candidate failed to make any inroads and the Communist Party candidate failed to win more than an eighth of the total votes cast, therefore losing his deposit.

In an article for the ILP paper, *Labour Leader*, the newly-elected MP gave his assessment of the election result: firstly giving his verdict on the

Morgan Jones soon after his by-election victory.
(Courtesy of Michael Thomas)

Communist campaign. He began magnanimously by stating that 'there is a case for Communism', although he went on to make his opinion known in no uncertain terms: 'But some of the 'stuff' doled out here simply defied description. It was unspeakably low in its tone, unfair in its insinuations, and quite dishonest in its intention'.[68]

In Morgan Jones' estimation, the Coalition was struggling from the start of the campaign:

'Their candidate was like a parrot that, after a course of patient training, had at last learnt to say two words – 'Lloyd George'. He seemed utterly bereft of any political ideas. And what was true of the candidate was true in the main of the supporters'.[69]

Jones' victory did not require a huge expenditure by the Labour Party. As the agent's election expenses show, just over £1,000 was spent in the campaign by the party. For a short campaign, this may appear a large amount for the time, but given the importance of the election one might have expected a larger sum. The largest expenditure was spent on literature (£332 0s 9d), followed by room hire for public meetings (£56 0s 6d).[70]

News of Morgan Jones' victory was enthusiastically received in the constituency, which he toured the following day – addressing a number of meetings – and it was reported that 'thousands' came out to welcome their new MP: in Caerphilly and Llanbradach there was even a local band accompanying him.[71]

The campaign had been a hard fight, but it had been worth it. Morgan Jones had made history. He had become the first conscientious objector to be elected a Member of Parliament and he had done so through an emphatic by-election victory. Despite huge efforts from the Coalition and Communist candidates, Jones had fought a calm and determined campaign which won huge support from the people of the Caerphilly constituency.

Notes

1. For good descriptions and explanations of the changing nature of the leadership, see Hywel Francis and David Smith, *The Fed. – a History of the South Wales Miners in the 20ᵗʰ Century*, (Lawrence and Wishart, 1980). Also Ness Edwards, *History of the South Wales Miners' Federation*, Vol. 1, (Lawrence and Wishart, 1938).

2. *Western Mail*, July 7ᵗʰ and 11ᵗʰ, 1921. *The Times*, July 7ᵗʰ, 1921. *South Wales Echo*, July 6ᵗʰ, 1921.

3. *Hansard*, the Official Parliamentary Record, contains very few references to Onions.

4. *Western Mail*, July 7ᵗʰ, 1921.

5. Ibid.

6. *Western Mail*, July 25ᵗʰ, 1921.

7. Ibid.

8. *Western Mail*, July 16ᵗʰ, 1921.

9. Ibid.

10. *Western Mail*, August 6ᵗʰ, 1921.

11. *Western Mail*, August 9ᵗʰ, 1921.

12. *Labour Leader*, September 1ˢᵗ, 1921.

13. *Caerphilly Journal*, April 30ᵗʰ, 1921.

14. James Klugmann, *History of the Communist Party of Great Britain 1919-1924*, (Lawrence and Wishart, 1987), pp.182-3.

15. See Wayne David, *Remaining True – A Biography of Ness Edwards*, (Caerphilly Local History Society, 2006), for a discussion of the issues which were shaping the politics of the Left at the time.

16. James Klugmann, op. cit., p.183.

17. *Caerphilly Journal*, August 20ᵗʰ, 1921.

18. James Klugmann, op. cit., p.183.

19. *Western Mail*, July 7ᵗʰ, 1921.

20. *Western Mail*, July 16ᵗʰ, 1921.

21. Ibid.

22. Various local authority records in the Glamorgan Archives, and F.W.S. Craig, *British Parliamentary Election Results: 1885-1922*, (Palgrave Macmillan, 1974).

23. Most of the UK-wide newspapers had extensive coverage of the short election campaign, as well as the coverage by the local and Welsh press.

24. The *Western Mail's* headlines, such as 'Mr Morgan Jones ignores the facts' and 'Labour's misguided tactics' give an indication of how the newspaper reported the election.

25. *Western Mail*, August 6ᵗʰ, 1921.

26. Ibid.

27. Quoted by James Klugmann, op. cit., p.183.
28. *Labour Leader*, September 1st, 1921.
29. Labour Party, annual conference report, 1922, p.56.
30. James Klugmann, op. cit., p.183.
31. Transcript of interview with Edgar Evans, November 30th, 1975: South Wales Miners' Library.
32. Robert Stewart, *Breaking the Fetters*, (Lawrence and Wishart, 1967), p.116.
33. James Klugmann, op. cit., p.183.
34. Ibid.
35. Jack Jones, *Unfinished Journey*, (Hamish Hamilton, 1937), p.198.
36. Ibid.
37. Ibid.
38. Robert Stewart, op. cit., p.116.
39. Ibid.
40. Robert Stewart, op. cit., p.117.
41. For a good introduction to the by-election, see Julie Cambridge, 'The Caerphilly by-election of 1921', *Journal of the Caerphilly Local History Society*, No. 7, 2004.
42. *Western Mail*, August 6th, 1921.
43. *Western Mail*, August 8th, 1921.
44. *Western Mail*, August 17th, 1921.
45. *Western Mail*, August 15th, 1921.
46. *Western Mail*, August 17th, 1921.
47. Labour Party, annual conference report, 1922, p.56.
48. See, for example, *Caerphilly Journal*, November 17th, 1914.
49. *Western Mail*, August 12th, 1921.
50. See, *Western Mail*, August 17th, 1921. Also *The Times*, August 26th, 1921.
51. *Western Mail*, August 20th, 1921.
52. *Western Mail*, August 22nd, 1921.
53. *Western Mail*, August 20th, 1921.
54. *Western Mail*, August 17th, 1921.
55. *Merthyr Express*, August 18th, 1921.
56. Ibid.
57. Ibid.
58. Ibid.
59. Ibid.
60. Ibid.
61. *Western Mail*, August 24th, 1921.
62. *The Times*, August 26th, 1921.
63. *Caerphilly Journal*, August 31st, 1921.
64. Ibid.
65. *Western Mail*, August 26th, 1921.
66. Ibid.
67. *The Times*, August 26th, 1921
68. *Labour Leader*, September 1st, 1921.
69. Ibid.
70. Summary of Election Expenses for Morgan Jones, London School of Economics, ILP/6/20/27.
71. *Caerphilly Journal*, August 31st, 1921.

4

MP and Education Minister

Unlike many of his fellow Labour parliamentary colleagues from south Wales, Morgan Jones believed that if MPs were to be effective parliamentarians they needed to be full-time MPs. He also thought they should be based in London with their families. Today, most Labour MPs are based in their constituencies but, in the 1920s, travel between Wales and London was time consuming, and Jones was determined to make the greatest possible use of parliament to bring about radical change. He firmly believed that this required total commitment to, and full participation in, the parliamentary process.[1]

This commitment to a full-time, London-based parliamentary career meant he and his wife moved to south east England. Jones had met Gladys Thomas when he was lay preaching in her chapel in Merthyr Tydfil after the First World War and, like him, Gladys was a school teacher. They married in 1923 and set-up

Morgan and Gladys with their eldest daughter, Brenda. (Courtesy of Nick Sheaff)

home in London: at first buying a 19th century house in Camberwell Road and later moving to Golders Green, before, in 1935, settling in a new house they had built on the eastern side of Hampstead Garden Suburb.[2] They named the house 'Vaynor' after the village near Merthyr Tydfil where Gladys had grown up. Designed by an architect, Jones apparently insisted on only one thing – that the house be white-washed to remind him of the cottage where he'd been born in Gelligaer.[3]

In 1925, Morgan and Gladys' first child, Brenda Mair, was born and three years later their second, Margaret Eluned arrived. Undoubtedly a loving father, Jones found it a constant annoyance that the pressure of political life prevented him from spending more time with his family.[4] Holidays with the family were cherished, and several were taken through the Workers' Travel Association, which organised visits for industrial workers. The late John Sheaff, Jones' son-in-law, explained however that Gladys did not find them entirely 'to her taste'.[5] Much more agreeable was the Mediterranean cruise which the family took in 1936. This, more luxurious, trip was paid for by the income from the lectures which he delivered to the other passengers on the history and politics of the places to be visited.[6]

Vaynor, the Jones family home in Norrice Lea, Hampstead. (Courtesy of Nick Sheaff)

The following year saw the family renting a cottage in Sussex, from where they visited Philip Snowden, and David Lloyd George whose home in Churt was nearby. The last family holiday was to St. Ives in Cornwall. On this occasion they met up with another Labour colleague, Arthur Jenkins – a fellow Welsh Labour MP – his wife Hattie and their son, the future MP and cabinet minister, Roy.[7]

Throughout Jones' political career, his wife Gladys was a constant source of support, encouragement and sound advice.[8] Gladys was very popular in the constituency and when, in 1929, the franchise was extended to include large numbers of women, Gladys played a major role in ensuring that the women of Caerphilly cast their vote for her husband.

Morgan Jones' two daughters, Margaret Eluned and Brenda Mair. (Courtesy of Nick Sheaff)

In Morgan Jones' 1929 election address, one of the four pages was devoted to an appeal from Gladys, 'To the Women Voters of the Caerphilly Division'. In her appeal, Gladys began by pointing-out that 'When the idea for votes for women was very unpopular...In this Division my husband was among the first to appear on the public platform in its support'. Gladys then went on to remind women voters that it was the 'Labour Movement' which had always wanted to honour motherhood and that it was the Labour Party which had 'consistently' stood for children's education and the 'protection' of young workers in their place of work. Tellingly, Gladys also stressed the importance of securing 'peace among nations' so that children should not become 'fodder for cannon'.[9]

Gladys' intervention, and the support of newly enfranchised women, certainly helped Jones increase his majority to 13,058 in the 1929 election.

Despite the constant political pressures, life in London was comfortable for the Jones family. Helped by an income from his occasional lecture tours in the United States, he and Gladys were able to engage a series of maids, all teenage girls from Wales,[10] and although the couple were never inclined to host political dinner parties, he did find time to play golf and tennis, but without being good at either. Gardening was also a great passion and his knowledge of roses was quite considerable.[11]

Throughout his political career Morgan Jones always found time to devote to his Christian beliefs, preaching in many chapels across the south of England

To the Women Voters of the Caerphilly Division.

My Dear Friends,

I venture to address to you an appeal for my husband, who is the Labour Candidate in the Caerphilly Parliamentary Division.

When the idea of votes for women was very unpopular, and when the other political parties would not touch it, the Labour Party was its strong supporter. In this Division my husband was among the first to appear on the public platform in its support.

We women are keenly interested in all problems where human life is concerned. Who should be more interested in child life than we who bear children? Ought we not to be active with the Labour Movement which has always wanted to honour motherhood?

The Labour Party has consistently stood for the protection of child life, and for the provision of nursery schools, ample recreation facilities, and a full opportunity of educational development. It has striven for the protection of young women workers in factories, workshops, and offices. It has always strenuously worked to secure peace among nations, so that our children shall not become fodder for cannon.

Because the Labour Party declares that human beings "shall have life and have it more abundantly" I ask for your cordial support for Mr. Morgan Jones.

Yours sincerely,

GLADYS JONES.

Gladys addressing the newly enfranchised women of Caerphilly. (Courtesy of Prof. Russell Deacon)

and south Wales, and was frequently a speaker at the annual meetings of the Baptist and Congregational Unions, as well as the Free Church Council. Jones also made the time to preach in his constituency; for example, he addressed the well-attended Young People's Rally at the Third Jubilee Celebrations at Tonyfelin Baptist Church in Caerphilly in 1934.[12] Like many devout Welsh Baptists, Jones was a committed teetotaller and often spoke at temperance gatherings.

Despite London now firmly being the centre of his political and personal focus, as the MP for Caerphilly Jones always did his utmost to maintain close links with Wales, the Rhymney Valley in particular, and regularly took visitors from his constituency on tours of the Palace of Westminster. In one recorded visit, he took five boys from his old school, Lewis School, Pengam, around parliament as part of their four-day visit to London in the summer of 1935.[13]

On his regular visits to Wales, Jones often saw his brothers and sisters and of course his mother, and throughout his time as Caerphilly's MP he never

Visiting Lewis School as an ex-pupil and the area's MP. (Western Mail) (Courtesy of the Western Mail)

Sarah Ann played a key role in Jones' political career.
(Courtesy of Michael Thomas)

failed to hold regular advice surgeries for his constituents. One of the venues for those surgeries being the front parlour of his now-widowed mother's home in Bargoed.[14]

In many ways, his mother, Sarah Ann, was Jones' essential link between the constituency and the 'hot house' of Westminster. She was especially close to him during his election campaigns, and one of his future political opponents was to recall Sarah Ann as a 'quaintly-dressed' elderly lady standing 'proudly by the side of her son' at one of Jones' election declarations. His opponent said that one of 'the most beautiful traits of his character' was his 'love and admiration of his mother', who he referred to as 'one of God's own saints'.[15]

Reflecting on Jones' life, a close political friend even went so far as to suggest that Sarah Ann was his 'standard bearer', and that her thoughts meant more to him 'than the opinions of statesmen, politicians or diplomats'. It was said that he would often ask, "What would mother say to all this, I wonder?"[16]

The importance he attached to his constituency, and his commitment to the people he represented, was always one of Morgan Jones' hallmarks. In his maiden speech, delivered on October 20th, 1921, Morgan Jones graphically demonstrated that his politics were firmly rooted in the experiences of the people of the Rhymney Valley. In his speech, Jones movingly spoke of the problem of unemployment and the miners who had suffered hardship during the recent lock-out; he drew MPs' attention to the fact that Glamorgan County Council, of which he was still a member, had provided "well over 1,000,000 meals for school children".[17] He then set out how local government was under enormous pressure trying to find the necessary finance to deal with the rising social pressures. As Jones progressed to the final part of his speech, he referred to ex-servicemen. After having stated that he was supported by "many hundreds of ex-servicemen" in his recent by-election,[18] something which gave him "the greatest pride", he made a biting attack on the prime minister. Only the previous day Lloyd George had suggested that ex-servicemen might "emigrate" to secure work, and Jones' comments could not have been more powerful. Of ex-servicemen, he said:

> "They had been taught to dream of a new Jerusalem. They had not anticipated, I am sure, that this new Jerusalem was to be founded on the prairies of Canada or in the bush of Australia. Neither do they desire that the new Jerusalem shall be pitched across the waters in order to make it more easy for the representatives of the old Jerusalem to remain unchallenged and unchallengeable in Lombard Street".*[19]

He concluded his maiden speech by referring to the "wolf of poverty and unemployment" now at the people's doors:

> "When they reach their homes after wearily wandering the public streets at eventide, they seem to hear them. I feel sure that, having closed their door upon their misery, as they thought, to be alone with it at their own fireside, they seem to hear the clawing of these wolves at their very doors. Sometimes they are on their hearths. I appeal to the government to do something, and that speedily, to bring some comfort, some contentment to the homes of the common people, that they may feel once more proud of their native land."[20]

During the following months and years Jones became a frequent parliamentary speaker, initially from the backbenches and then the frontbench. A familiar figure, at all time wearing his distinctive bow tie, his speeches and interventions were invariably authoritative yet moderate in tone and content. Because of this, Jones drew respect from both sides of the commons.[21]

In his first couple of years as an MP, Jones spoke on many occasions and, as one would expect, his speeches reflected his values and his experiences. He spoke eloquently about the need for international disarmament, the importance of school meals, the desirability of self-government for the colonies, and the importance of helping the less well-off. He was also a strong opponent of the government's proposal to extend the disenfranchisement of

---

*   Lombard Street was the traditional banking street in London.

conscientious objectors and, as a foretaste of his future interest in the Middle East, was an early advocate of a new Jewish state.[22] Importantly, the newly elected MP expressed his serious concern about developments in Russia in a European context, and in 1922 he movingly asked the House of Commons to:

> *"Imagine a Bolshevik child in the midst of poverty and hunger, the gaunt spectre of disease standing at its very elbow, appealing to the prime minister of the leading nation of the world and the most civilised – so they say! – appealing for food, and the prime minister turning on him and saying 'Ah, my boy, I am very sympathetic with you but, as you know, I am teaching your father a lesson!' That is the most pitiless language I think I have ever heard, and the most disgraceful".[23]*

In the general election of 1922, Jones set out his appeal in a no-holds-barred manifesto. He reminded his electors that in the previous year he had successfully stood 'as a Labour candidate holding socialist convictions'. Now, he said, 'Toryism, naked and unashamed, challenges my return. The faces of class snobbery, class privilege, and class bias are organising to defeat the onward march of democracy'.[24]

First and foremost in his manifesto, he placed international issues. In particular, his support for the League of Nations and his commitment to 'self-government of the Irish people'. He also outlined his domestic priorities, which included 'social' measures to assist the unemployed and senior citizens, the nationalisation of the mines and railways, and an increase in the taxation of land and wealth.[25]

In a straight, two-way fight with the Conservative and Unionist candidate, he romped home with an increased majority and 57% of the vote. Caerphilly was undoubtedly now a very safe Labour seat.

Following the 1922 election, Jones' contributions to parliamentary debates became a little less frequent after he was appointed a Junior Opposition Whip.[26] In 1923, he was elected to the Labour Party's National Executive Committee (NEC), and when the 18 Welsh Labour MPs decided to form a Welsh group of the Parliamentary Labour Party (PLP), it was Morgan Jones who they elected as their first secretary.[27]

All of Wales' Labour MPs gave their full support to the miners in the 1926 General Strike and the six months lock-out which followed. Representing a mining constituency, Morgan Jones was acutely aware of the hardship which the miners and their families were suffering as the lock-out dragged on through what the Rhymney Valley poet, Idris Davies, called in his *Gwalia Deserta* the 'long hot summer of soup and speeches'.

Throughout the valley, fundraising events were organised to maintain the innumerable soup kitchens and in Virginia Park, Caerphilly, for example, a

Morgan Jones meeting St. John's Ambulance volunteers at Caerphilly Castle during the late 1920s. (Courtesy of Michael Thomas)

Monster Cup Carnival was held in October.[28] This saw no fewer than 20 jazz, comic and gazooka bands performing after they had marched around the town. Male voice parties, from a number of villages and from some chapels, also toured around England, bringing back much needed funds for the soup kitchens.[29]

As the lock-out dragged on into the summer, though, it became increasingly clear that a compromise was needed to bring the dispute to an end. In July, he strongly supported the so-called Bishops' Proposals and urged the Welsh miners to follow the advice of the MFGB executive and vote for the acceptance of the proposals. However, pit head meetings were held rather than a ballot vote and the proposals were rejected, with the two largest coalfields – Yorkshire and south Wales – tipping the balance. Jones was dismayed and he made it clear that 'the miners had committed an error of judgment' in not accepting the proposals 'as a basis for negotiations'. Nevertheless, he hoped that the miners would continue to 'stand firm', but be ready 'to explore every avenue for an honourable peace'.[30]

Morgan Jones expressed his contentious views in a number of meetings the length and breadth of the Rhymney Valley. His views were strongly challenged by the Caerphilly division's Labour Party organiser, and by members of the Communist Party and Miners' Minority Movement. At a meeting in Abertridwr, he spent nearly an hour responding to 'a varying fire of questions' from communist activists. Relations between Jones and the Communist Party had been poor since his by-election victory, and his exasperation was clearly evidenced by his comment that "it was not only time to sweep the Communist cobweb out of the district, but it was time to kill the spider as well."

Jones' views were also strongly criticised within the local Labour Party. Particularly vociferous was Claude Denscombe, the Labour Party organiser in Caerphilly and Morgan Jones' election agent. Denscombe was deeply involved in the efforts to raise money for the miners and was of the opinion that Jones ought not to question the miners' strategy.[31]

Even though Jones wanted the miners to return to work with a dignified compromise, he continued to give whatever support he could to the efforts of the miners to sustain themselves. His support was also very political and this was demonstrated clearly when he played a leading role in an important meeting at the Carmel Congregational Chapel in Fochriw, in the northern end of the Rhymney Valley, after the lock-out in December 1926. The meeting was organised to pay tribute to nine men and two women who had been released from prison after serving their sentences for their part in a so-called 'riot'. Jones paid tribute to them and, along with local 'Fed' leaders, he presented the men with inscribed gold cigarette cases and the women with necklaces and gold pendants. '1926' was a statement of coalfield solidarity and no one recognised this more than Morgan Jones.[32]

In Westminster, education was Jones' main initial interest as a Member of Parliament, and where he had his biggest impact. Because of his experience, Jones was an obvious choice to be an education spokesman for Labour and he was asked to join the party's Advisory Committee on Education soon after he was elected.[33] From the moment of his election, Jones had shown a passionate concern for the education of all and, as Rodney Barker noted, he 'brought to his thinking about educational policy the practical mind of a teacher who wished to give general currency to particular virtues which he already detected in the educational system'.[34]

The Labour Party published *Secondary Education for All* in 1922, a policy paper largely drafted by the prominent educationalist and Christian socialist R.H. Tawney, which argued for full-time secondary education for all young people up to the age of 16. Rather than just advocating an expansion of education, however, the task which Labour's education team in the commons had to grapple with was also how best to oppose the draconian education spending cuts being introduced by the Coalition government.[35]

The responsibility of leading for the opposition on the third reading of the bill, which was to introduce these cuts, fell to Morgan Jones. He told MPs, in no uncertain terms, "you cannot bring the ethics and practices of the counting house into the elementary schools or into the secondary schools".[36] In an equally trenchant way, he opposed the suggestion that there should be an increase in the teacher-pupil ratio and what he called "the monstrous proposition" to close primary schools with under 100 pupils.[37] For Jones, it was wrong that the well-off should deprive the children of those who were less well-off to access to literature,

On a family seaside holiday in 1934. (Courtesy of Nick Sheaff)

the arts and science. What was needed, he argued, was not a retrenchment of education but an expansion.[38]

In another debate, the following month, Jones set out his alternative to the government's cuts. Central to his approach was the principle of equality; he did not believe that there was an educational justification for a division between the elementary and secondary schools – a division which saw the children of middle class parents going to the latter and working class children to the former.[39]

Morgan Jones did however add a qualification: rather than advocate a straightforward single system for all secondary pupils, he appeared to suggest that for a child to be transferred from an elementary school to a secondary one, they first had to show evidence of 'intellectual capacity'. He also displayed a respect for, and indeed almost an admiration of, the standards of public schools. This has led to some suggestions that Jones had an 'elitist' view of education.[40] To be fair, however, as Dylan Rees has argued,[41] he did not favour the maintenance of the public school sector but wanted the small class sizes and high educational standards of the public schools transferred to the state schools so that all young people could have the same opportunities. It is also important to bear in mind that at this stage, Jones' ideas were still very much in gestation.

When Ramsay MacDonald formed a minority Labour government in January 1924, Sir Charles Trevelyan, a recent convert from the Liberals, was appointed president of the Board of Education and Morgan Jones was made his deputy as secretary to the board.[42] The relationship between the two was not good, and apparently Trevelyan was not impressed by Jones, although the Fabian, Beatrice Webb, accurately described Morgan Jones in her diary as one of the government's 'lower middle-class brainworkers'.[43] His appointment was, though, generally welcomed in the parliamentary party because there

Morgan Jones, as education minister, with fashion students at Barrett Street School, London, circa 1930. (Courtesy of London College of Fashion)

was widespread recognition of his practical experience in education and his effectiveness in the chamber. To become a government minister barely three years after being elected was testimony in itself to the high regard in which he was held. Jones was delighted to join the government and told the *Merthyr Express* that he was looking forward to his post because he saw education, "as a broad highway on which all who so desired could walk without hardship or difficulty".[44]

Unfortunately for Jones, however, Ramsay MacDonald's government did not last long. It was in office for less than 10 months and Morgan Jones' time as a minister was largely taken up with trying to resolve disagreements in Wales over the inspection of secondary education: there was a dispute between the Central Welsh Board (CWB) and the Welsh Department of the Board of Education, both of which had a role in school inspection. The CWB was determined to resist the Welsh Department's pressure to move towards a single Welsh inspectorate and Jones put in a great deal of effort trying to resolve the dispute. As the CWB believed the Board was trying to exploit its financial difficulties, Jones proposed an increase in its centrally allocated grant. He hoped that this would help to persuade the CWB to accept some curtailment of their independence.[45]

In a speech in Llandudno, Jones also raised the possibility of devolving education in Wales to a Welsh National Council for Education. Although neither he nor the government were in a position to make any hard and fast promises because of the government's minority position, there can be no doubt that he saw an opportunity to open a new chapter in Welsh education.[46] This was confirmed when Jones sent a memorandum to Trevelyan stating that the creation of a National Council should be the next step in the development of education policy in Wales.[47]

His ground-breaking suggestion, as well as the agreement he was trying to broker on the Welsh examination inspection system, ultimately came to nothing as the government soon fell after losing a vote of no confidence. However, in suggesting that education policy in Wales should be devolved and run on an all-Wales basis, Morgan Jones was well ahead of his time. It would be many years before a Welsh Office was established and the first tentative moves made towards a distinctive Welsh educational policy.

During the 1920s, an issue which took up much of Jones' time and effort was the attempts of the Communist Party to influence Labour's education policy. The CP was, at this time, making a concerted effort to infiltrate the Labour Party and, from his by-election experience, Jones was only too aware of CP tactics. Knowing what was happening in local Labour parties in different parts of the country, he felt he had a duty to take the lead in thwarting the CPGB's 'entryism' of the Labour Party and its attempt to gain control of the leading progressive teaching organisation the Teachers' Labour League (TLL).[48]

The TLL had been established in 1923 to encourage teachers into the Labour Party and to help develop Labour's education policy. Jones became the TLL's parliamentary secretary, but it soon faced difficulties when it became a target for the CP and began to adopt increasingly far-left positions. At the Labour Party's 1926 conference, its representatives persuaded party delegates to support a resolution which condemned 'reactionary and imperialistic teaching in the schools, particularly with regard to Empire Day celebrations and the use of history and other textbooks with an anti-working class bias'.[49]

The communists also attempted to secure conference support for the National Council of Labour Colleges (NCLC), the Marxist adult education organisation. This resolution was only defeated after Jones, on behalf of the NEC, had argued that the resolution should be rejected as it would favour the NCLC over the mainstream Workers' Educational Association (WEA).

*On holiday with Gladys, Margaret and Brenda in 1935.
(Courtesy of Nick Sheaff)*

For Jones, this was the final straw. At the league's fifth annual conference, he and 14 other like-minded colleagues left the organisation. As an alternative to the TLL, a break-away group set-up a new organisation known as the National Association of Labour Teachers (NALT). This became an effective body which championed equality of educational opportunity and which argued the case for educational issues generally to be given a higher profile in the party. Their work was in stark contrast to the now communist-dominated TLL, which argued for rigidly ideological, pro-working class school syllabuses. Morgan Jones was heavily involved in the early meetings of the NALT and was, in effect, the group's mentor.[50]

Given his stand, the Communist Party and its fellow travellers launched a ferocious and personal counter-attack on Jones. A letter was sent to all the Labour movement organisations in the Caerphilly constituency accusing Jones of forming a 'blackleg organisation' and asking the local Labour Party to examine its MP's conduct.[51] The circular had the desired effect and prompted some sharp criticism of Jones by members of his own party in Caerphilly.[52]

The conflict between the TLL and the Labour leadership came to a head at the party's 1927 conference. None other than the leader of the party, Ramsay MacDonald, explained to conference that the NEC has decided to disaffiliate the TLL because of the Communist Party's influence within it and because of the campaign which they inspired against Morgan Jones in his own constituency. In a highly heated debate, Jones vigorously defended himself against charges that he was a 'Spencer or a Hodge'.* The conference gave Jones its full support.[53]

Relations between the Labour Party and the Communist Party were difficult throughout this period. The Labour Party was concerned about

---

* Both George Spencer and Frank Hodges were despised in the Labour movement. Spencer because he was the founder of 'blackleg' trade unions and Hodges because he had 'betrayed' the miners and had now been appointed to the Central Electricity Board.

entryism and was worried about the Communist Party promoting its agenda through 'front' organisations, and on at least one occasion alerted Morgan Jones to the fact that 'auxiliary organisations of the 3rd International' were trying to recruit members in Britain. Having been made aware of the true nature of an organisation called Friends of the Chinese People, Jones assured the party's general secretary that he would withdraw from speaking at one of their conferences.[54]

In 1929, Labour formed a minority government for the second time. Once again, Charles Trevelyan was appointed president of the Board of Education and Jones was made parliamentary secretary. Surprisingly, we know from his private papers that Trevelyan was still not enthusiastic about Morgan Jones and only accepted his appointment with some reluctance.[55]

Soon after the government was formed, Trevelyan secured the unenthusiastic agreement of cabinet for the raising of the school leaving age to 15, from April 1st, 1929, and for the introduction of maintenance grants. Morgan Jones was heavily involved in the Board of Education discussions about how best to proceed, and although Jones' influence in the short term was probably quite limited, as Dylan Rees has argued,[56] his interventions helped shape policy in the long term. Jones was now committed to what were known at the time as 'multi-bias' schools: secondary schools which had a broad geographic coverage but with differing curriculums.[57] In many ways, it can be argued Jones was beginning to move towards a vision of 'comprehensive' secondary schooling, although he still favoured independent schools in certain parts of the country.

The educational record of Ramsay Macdonald's second Labour government is, on balance, not at all positive. While the number of certified teachers increased, the numbers of classes with over 50 children was reduced, and a variety of measures introduced to advance equality and opportunity, these achievements have to be set against the failure of the government's flagship Education Bill. The sorry story of this piece of draft legislation began with the cabinet displaying a marked lack of enthusiasm. It then experienced delay and procrastination and was subjected to internal opposition. In the end, it was the victim of debilitating division within the PLP.[58]

Some have suggested that Ramsay MacDonald himself was far from convinced of the bill's central proposal – the raising of the school leaving age[59] – and the proposed introduction of maintenance grants proved to be particularly contentious within the PLP. Snowden, the Chancellor, had concerns about cost, and in the party generally there was widespread apprehension about means testing: for many, means testing was a way of creating unfairness and was therefore iniquitous. In the House of Commons, Morgan Jones stoutly defended the bill, emphasising its educational worth,[60] but the bill was

Jones pictured, when secretary of the Board of Education, after laying the foundation stone for Snapethorpe Elementary School in Wakefield, West Yorkshire in 1930. (Courtesy of British Pathé News)

withdrawn by the government before it went to the vote after the debate at second reading.

Soon after, the government tried again with another bill, and this time the bill passed its second reading with Jones replying to the debate. Referring to the opposition's attitude to the bill, he stated, "they take the view that this bill will be a millstone round the necks of the people of this country. We take the view that it is a milestone".[61] Essentially, however, the bill was little different to its predecessor and significant opposition again came from Labour's own ranks. Much to the Tories' glee, this time there was an amendment during report stage from a Roman Catholic senior backbench Labour MP. The amendment proposed delaying the implementation of the bill until there had been financial provision made for the voluntary sector schools, and the Tories happily fell in behind the Labour rebels. The amendment was prompted by a concern about the potential cost implication which would, it was argued, fall on Catholic, Anglican and other non-provided schools. Trevelyan had proposed a concession which was likely to have seen-off the rebellion but this was vetoed by Ramsay MacDonald, and in the subsequent vote a significant defeat was inflicted on the government.[62]

Trevelyan had now had enough. In exasperation with MacDonald's leadership as much as anything, he tendered his resignation from the government in March 1931. Perhaps Morgan Jones might have thought he had a claim to the post, but Trevelyan was succeeded by Lees-Smith, another convert from the Liberals, and Jones remained in his position until the general election five months later. Despite Jones' undoubted commitment, there could be no disguising the fact that, with a total of two failed Education bills and the resignation of the president of the Board of Education, Labour's attempt at educational reform had failed.

Morgan Jones was never to hold ministerial office again. When Ramsay MacDonald turned his back on the Labour Party to form a National government and Trevelyan lost his seat in Newcastle in the 1931 general election, Jones became Labour's education spokesman. In a very much smaller PLP, he stood out as a shining star and the *Western Mail* even tipped him as a possible future prime minister.[63] Now, without the stresses and strains of government, Jones was able to give more thought to policy development.

In July 1930, Trevelyan had established a special committee tasked to look into 'The Educational Problems of the South Wales Coalfield', with particular reference to the provision of technical and cultural education. As Morgan Jones had pressed hard for such an inquiry, he was the obvious choice to be its chairman,[64] and when the committee reported – in the winter of 1931 – it reflected in large part Jones' own thinking about the policies which were needed to reverse south Wales' economic fortunes. The report stated that the region's industrial base needed to be 'broadened' and 'technical education' needed to be 're-orientated, broadened in scope and raised in standard'. More co-operation between schools and industry was advocated and it suggested the creation of a South Wales Advisory Council for Further Education.[65]

Much of the report has a familiar ring today but, unfortunately, many of its recommendations were either only nominally welcomed or ignored completely by the newly-elected National government. Yet, as mass unemployment increasingly disfigured the coalfield communities, the report's central proposal was more relevant than ever before. It argued strongly that so-called 'technical' education needed to be central to a modern economy, and Jones himself said to the House of Commons, "I am absolutely sure that if there is a gap in our educational system at this moment it is on the technical education side".[66]

Morgan Jones had a huge admiration for the United States and undertook a number of lecture tours in the country during parliamentary recesses, many in the company of fellow lecturing companion Rhys J. Davies, the MP for Westhoughton in Lancashire.[67] It was during his visits to the United States that Jones became increasingly convinced of the need for more and better technical education and, after Labour had lost power in 1924, he travelled particularly widely in the States and visited many schools and other educational institutions. As a result, Jones came to believe that it was essential for Britain to learn from the American experience and, as he told the House of Commons in April 1929:

"I am absolutely convinced that if our country is to hold her own in the great fight for commercial priority among the nations of the world, she must develop her technical education to an infinitely greater degree ... it is quite certain that Americans appreciate to a considerable degree, and much more than we do, the necessity for the development of technical education".[68]

When the National government was formed in 1931, its education policy consisted of one thing only – reducing expenditure – a strategy resolutely opposed by Jones. At the 1932 Labour Party conference he strongly attacked the cuts policy, arguing that what was needed was a new child-centred policy.[69] Significantly, he also indicated that he could no longer support the policy of so-called secondary schools for the children of the well-to-do, while children whose parents could not afford to pay would go to central schools.[70]

Jones' ideas on education at this time were firmed-up through discussions he had with the New Fabian Research Bureau (NFRB), and in May 1934 he wrote three papers for the bureau.[71] The first paper argued strongly for the raising of the school leaving age from 14 to 15, a proposal which had failed under the second Labour government. In support of his case, Jones marshalled a range of expert opinions, including a social survey of Merseyside and the recently published Hadow* Report.

The paper also attacked 'the menace of juvenile unemployment' and the government's plan for Junior Instruction Centres, which Jones predicted would be expensive and inefficient. The way forward, he suggested, was set out by Sir Percy Jackson, the chairman of the West Riding Education Committee, who said in his presidential address to the North of England Education conference, "I suggest that the minister of labour can halve the problem, and more than halve his cost, if the government will raise the school-leaving age to 15".[72]

---

*   Sir W.H. Hadow was a leading educational reformer and musicologist.

The second paper focussed on what would be a future Labour government's educational programme. Again written in May 1934, the paper's starting point was that the 'consideration' turned mainly on the 'problems of finance'.[73] Jones believed there would be many demands on a future Labour government, from 'social services' in particular, and there would be the likelihood that a future Labour Government would devote a great deal of legislative time to 'the nationalisation of one or more of the great industries'. It therefore followed that those departments, like the Board for Education, which were 'already sufficiently endowed with legislative authority' ought to implement as much legislation as possible without congesting parliament with bills.[74]

Following on from what he had said in his first paper, Jones argued that the one exception for fresh legislation would be a bill for the raising of the school leaving age. He recognised, though, that there was still a great deal of opposition to this inside the Labour Party and therefore to preserve party unity he believed it would be a good idea if the issue was delayed until the latter stages of the government's life.

Well before a formal raising of the school leaving age, Jones favoured the introduction of free secondary education. This, he believed, would not cost the state that much more than raising the school leaving age. There would also be the important advantage that by introducing free secondary education it would remove the incentive for children of working class parents to be taken out of school.

Other radical proposals in Morgan Jones' second paper included the introduction of nursery schools, a reduction in class sizes, the construction of new buildings in elementary schools, the introduction of playing fields and physical exercise for children in elementary as well as secondary schools, new technical schools and better teacher training. This last proposal was given some weight because Jones' third NFRB paper provided important facts and figures relating to teacher training.[75]

On the issue of private schools, Jones thought they were 'shockingly inefficient', but as he was reluctant to open another contentious issue he thought that it was an issue that ought not to be tackled 'at this stage'. Importantly, he also gave a clear indication of how his thinking was developing when he stated that he was strongly in favour of 'a multiple bias 11 plus school' as this would allow the academically and practically minded to be educated in the same school.[76]

This last point provided a marker which was to assume greater significance as the debate about educational opportunity gathered momentum. Morgan Jones was now beginning to move to the view that a more radical education policy ought to be developed and advocated by the Labour Party. In June

1935, during a Board of Education Supply Committee, he set out a vision of education which later became described as 'comprehensive'. Although he did not use the term comprehensive, there is little doubt that he was coming to the settled view that the binary divide in secondary education was outmoded and not appropriate to the modern, more equal society which he wanted to see. In that debate he stated:

> *"I refer to the scheme of having one school at which all children of 11 plus will attend, a school so big that both the practically-minded children and the academically-minded children will go through the same portals, a school which will provide a curriculum for the one and a curriculum for the other under the same roof, so that the child who is practically-minded shall not feel that he has been shoved into some place less meritorious academically than that in to which the academically-minded child has been put."*[77]

By the late 1930s, the Labour Party was beginning to rekindle its interest in education and the creation of a new Education Advisory Committee (EAC) in 1938 was clear evidence of this. Under Jones' chairmanship, the committee began to 'investigate' and report on education policy with a view to preparing major new policy documents.[78] Soon after the EAC started meeting, a sub-committee was formed consisting of Morgan Jones, R.H. Tawney, the prominent Fabian, Barbara Drake, and the radical, young academic Brian Simon.[79] This was a high-powered group and its influence upon centre-left thinking over the next few years, and especially after the Second World War, was to be significant. Sadly, Morgan Jones' early death meant that he did not play a role in the group's work, but its establishment was due, in no small part, to his determined efforts.

Notes

1.   John Sheaff, *Morgan Jones – a Memorial*, op. cit., p.18. Also Rhys J. Davies MP, *An Appreciation*, and the personal papers of Margaret Sheaff.
2.   John Sheaff, op. cit.
3.   Ibid, and in conversation with John and Margaret Sheaff, summer 2015.
4.   John Sheaff, op. cit.
5.   Conversation with John and Margaret Sheaff, summer 2015.
6.   John Sheaff, op. cit., p.18.
7.   John Sheaff, op. cit., pp.18-19.
8.   Conversation with John and Margaret Sheaff, summer 2015.
9.   Election Address, 1929. I am grateful to Prof. R. Deacon for a copy of this.
10.   John Sheaff. op. cit., p.19.

11. Ibid. Also conversation with John and Margaret Sheaff, summer 2015.

12. H.P. Richards, *Tonyfelin Welsh Baptist Church, Caerphilly: 1784-1984*, (self-published, 1985), p.48.

13. Ewart Smith, *Lewis' School, Pengam - A History*, (Old Bakehouse Publications, 2013), pp.75-6.

14. Conversation with John and Margaret Sheaff, summer. 2015.

15. *Western Mail*, April 26th, 1939.

16. John Sheaff, op. cit., p.2.

17. *Hansard*, October 20th, 1921, col. 351.

18. *Hansard*, October 20th, 1921, col. 354.

19. *Hansard*, October 20th, 1921, col. 354-355.

20. *Hansard*, October 20th, 1921, col. 355.

21. John Sheaff, op. cit., p.4.

22. See *Hansard* during the autumn of 1921 and early 1922.

23. *Hansard*, July 26th, 1922, cols. 581-582.

24. Election Address 1922, London School of Economics, ILP/6/20/27.

25. Ibid.

26. *Who's Who of British Members of Parliament, Vol. III, 1919-1945*, (Harvester Press, 1979).

27. Chris Williams, *Oxford Dictionary of National Biography*, (Oxford University Press, 2004).

28. *Caerphilly Journal*, October 23rd, 1926.

29. *Caerphilly Journal*, October 30th, 1926. Also see minute book of Caerphilly Workmen's Hall and Institute for 1926 to 1928, (still held by the Hall Committee).

30. *Merthyr Express*, August 14th, 1926.

31. Ibid.

32. *Merthyr Express*, December 18th, 1926.

33. Referred to by Dylan Rees, 'Morgan Jones, Educationalist and Labour Politician', *Morgannwg*, Vol. XXXI, 1987, p.71.

34. Rodney Barker, *Education and Politics, 1900-1951: A Study of the Labour Party*, (Clarendon Press, 1972), pp.104-5.

35. Dylan Rees, 'Morgan Jones: Educationalist and Labour Politician', op. cit., p.71.

36. *Hansard*, March 28th, 1922, Vol. 152, col. 1170.

37. Ibid.

38. Dylan Rees, 'Morgan Jones: Educationalist and Labour Politician', op. cit., p.72.

39. *Hansard*, April 27th, 1922, Vol. 153, col. 839.

40. Rodney Barker, op. cit., pp.104-105.

41. Dylan Rees, 'Morgan Jones: Educationalist and Labour Politician', op. cit., p.71.

42. Dylan Rees, 'Morgan Jones: Educationalist and Labour Politician', op. cit.,p.72.

43. Cited by Dylan Rees, 'Morgan Jones: Educationalist and Labour Politician', op. cit., p.81. from *The Diaries of Beatrice Webb*. Vol. 11. p.210.

44. *Merthyr Express*, November 6th, 1924.

45. Dylan Rees, 'Morgan Jones: Educationalist and Labour Politician', op. cit., pp.72-74.

46. Ibid., p.73.

47. Ibid.

48. See Wayne David, 'The Labour Party and the "exclusion" of the Communists; the case of the Ogmore Divisional Labour Party in the 1920s', *Llafur* (The Journal for the Study of Welsh Labour History) Vol.3, No.4, 1995, for another example of the CP's tactics.

49. Dylan Rees, 'Morgan Jones: Educationalist and Labour Politician', op. cit., p.74.

50. Dylan Rees, 'Morgan Jones: Educationalist and Labour Politician', op. cit., p.75.

51. Dylan Rees, 'Morgan Jones: Educationalist and Labour Politician', op. cit., p.82.

52. *Caerphilly Journal*, April 23rd, 1927.
53. Labour Party, annual conference report, 1927.
54. Correspondence from Morgan Jones to the Labour Party general secretary, ID/C1/53/8-7-14-8-11-10, Museum of People's History, Manchester.
55. Dylan Rees, 'Morgan Jones: Educationalist and Labour Politician', op. cit., p.76.
56. Ibid.
57. Ibid.
58. Dylan Rees, 'Morgan Jones: Educationalist and Labour Politician', op. cit., p.77.
59. Rodney Barker, op. cit., p.105.
60. Dylan Rees, 'Morgan Jones: Educationalist and Labour Politician', op. cit., p.77.
61. *Hansard*, November 6th, 1930, Vol. 244, col. 1194.
62. Rodney Barker, op. cit., p.106.
63. *Western Mail*, November 29th, 1932.
64. Dylan Rees, 'Morgan Jones: Educationalist and Labour Politician', op. cit., p.78.
65. Ibid.
66. Ibid.
67. Rhys J. Davies, *The Late Morgan Jones*, op. cit., pp.1-5.
68. *Hansard*, April 23rd, 1929, col. 763.
69. Labour Party, annual conference report, 1932.
70. Ibid.
71. New Fabian Research Bureau, LJ39/4, London School of Economics.
72. Ibid.
73. Ibid.
74. Ibid.
75. Ibid.
76. Ibid.
77. *Hansard*, June 17th, 1935, cols 137-138.
78. Dylan Rees, *Dictionary of Labour Biography*, op. cit., p.149.
79. Ibid.

5

Westminster and Wales

Today, it is difficult to fully comprehend the enormity of Labour's electoral defeat in 1931 and the profound impact it had on the party. Only a handful of Labour MPs had followed their leader, Ramsay MacDonald, when he formed a National government in 1931 and, in the general election that followed, Labour's representation was reduced from 246 seats to a mere 52. Its heaviest defeats were in the English Midlands and Scotland; in Greater London 45 seats were lost and, beyond London, the south of England failed to return a single Labour MP.

In Wales, Labour fared a little better with its representation falling from 25 to 16 seats. In Caerphilly, where Morgan Jones was loyal to the Labour Party, only a Conservative stood against him and Labour's majority was a healthy 12,017.[1]

It was not only the number of MPs which Labour lost across Britain, it was also the calibre of those MPs. No fewer than 14 cabinet members and 21 other frontbenchers and party whips lost their seats. Close to a generation of the brightest and best were taken out of the political arena: many never to return to parliament. Of those who remained, only about 30 were effective parliamentarians.

There was, therefore, a huge responsibility on those who now made up the 'rump' of the PLP, with the leader of the opposition's office being shared by Stafford Cripps, Clem Attlee and George Lansbury.[2] Their life was not made easier by the increasingly fractious handful of ILP MPs who frequently flouted the Labour whip. By the time the ILP left the Labour Party in 1932, Jones and the ILP had long since parted company, and he was now firmly in the political centre of the Labour Party; radical and progressive, but always rational, loyal and constructive.[3]

In the aftermath of Labour's crushing defeat, Jones now took on an additional and important position. Because of the small number of Labour MPs, he combined his role as Labour's education's spokesman with chairmanship of the extremely important Parliamentary Committee of Public Accounts

Morgan Jones during the mid-1930s. (Courtesy of Nick Sheaff)

(which we would today call a Select Committee). He held this position, which was unpaid, from 1931 until his death.[4]

The role of the committee was to ensure that the government was effectively held to account for its actions in all areas of public expenditure. Its purpose, therefore, was not to 'shadow' any single government department, but to have a roving brief over all areas of public expenditure. Given that, by now, Jones commanded respect on both sides of the house, he was in many ways ideally suited for a post that was not party political.[5]

The responsibilities involved in chairing this committee were huge and meant that when parliament was in session, Jones had to sit in a 'special room', interviewing and cross-examining the heads of various government departments about their expenditure plans. The normal schedule for such days meant conducting such interviews from 11am until 5pm.[6]

One of the issues which Jones tackled quickly was the long-standing concern that governments were avoiding the necessity of obtaining parliamentary approval for some areas of expenditure. This was being done by making use of the Contingencies Fund, and therefore obviating the need to obtain statutory approval for specific areas of expenditure. To deal with this, Jones insisted on the 1932 Committee of Public Accounts 'concordat'. This established the general rule that continuing functions of government should be defined in specific statute. Only 'certain recognised exceptions' to this general principle were to be permitted.[7]

This became immediately relevant because, in November 1931, the National government cut the rates of unemployment benefit and introduced a new means test, by using two orders-in-council, which altered primary legislation through secondary legislation, thereby bypassing the established legislative route. The use of so-called Henry VIII clauses meant that the government had been able to avoid much parliamentary debate and scrutiny of an extremely controversial measure.[8] Morgan Jones' new concordat meant that future governments would find it very difficult to introduce financial measures in such a way again. It holds firm to this day.

Another innovation introduced during his time as chairman of the Public Accounts Committee was an extension of the committee's responsibilities for scrutiny. In 1934 it secured an extension of its terms of reference to enable it to consider 'such other accounts laid before parliament as the committee may think fit'.[9]

The National government's spending cuts and its economic policy, followed from 1935 by those of Stanley Baldwin's Conservatives, were hugely resented by working people across Britain and nothing drew as much hostility as the hated means test. This was the investigation families had to endure before they could receive unemployment benefit. It meant that any form of income, including pensions, savings, the earnings of other family members, and even household possessions had to be declared. The resentment felt by people across the south Wales coalfield was huge and it was hardly surprising that in 1932 Caerphilly Town Council passed a resolution calling for the abolition of the hated means test.[10]

During this period unemployment was increasing rapidly, such as when, in March 1928, the Aber Valley experienced a particularly harsh blow with the closure of the largest colliery in the area, the Universal Colliery in Senghenydd, and 2,600 jobs were lost.[11] Unemployment in the 1930s meant destitution, and a local historian commented, with good reason, that 'unemployment not only seared the soul' but affected people's diet and health. Potatoes, bread and margarine replaced a balanced diet of meat, eggs and milk. Rickets and tuberculosis increased and infant mortality worsened.[12]

In a debate on the new unemployment assistance regulations, in July 1936, which introduced means testing, Jones provided the House of Commons with a graphic example of the hardship that was now being caused in the Welsh coalfield:

"Last Saturday I heard a working-class woman make a speech at Cardiff. She made a better speech than I could ever hope to make, for she told her own story. She said that she had a neighbour who had a sick daughter among a number of children. The doctor had told her, 'Take your child up to the top of the mountain for fresh air, and when she comes down give her eggs and milk.' What was the reply? The woman said: 'I can't do it. If I give this one eggs and milk, the younger one will want the same, and I can't afford it.' That is a human story, a story of happenings in a working-class home, under existing conditions."[13]

In the same debate, Jones stated that he was especially concerned about the effect of the means test on young people:

"The worst that can be said and the biggest criticism that can be made of the regulations is their effect upon youth. When my Hon. Friends and I come up from south Wales on Monday mornings from Bridgend, [Port] Talbot, Cardiff or Newport, they see a steady stream of young people coming from these areas up to London or to other large cities".[14]

Defeat for Labour at the end of the debate was inevitable, but he concluded his speech in a powerful and determined way:

"I warn the Right Hon. Gentleman and the government that, though we are beaten tomorrow night in the Division Lobby, the fight against these regulations must go on, for we cannot accept the standardisation of these benefits and the placing of them permanently upon the shoulders of our people. We shall carry on this fight, and in the long run right will triumph over wrong, and those who do the work of this country will enter into their share of the recompense."[15]

Although Jones' new role restricted his participation in the political activity of the Chamber, he did nevertheless contribute to the annual debates following the Budget. In 1935 he reminded MPs, by way of a Dickensian analogy, of what the Chancellor had said following his 'doctor's mandate' in 1931, which had led to swathing public spending cuts. His speech questioned the effectiveness of the government's whole economic approach:

"Three years ago the Chancellor of the Exchequer was inviting us to leave 'Bleak House' and to entertain 'Great Expectations'. The day before yesterday he seemed to have abandoned those 'Great Expectations' and we were most clearly back on the way towards 'Bleak House'... Three years ago he was basking in the uncertain glory of an April day; Which now shews all the beauty of the sun, but two days ago he was conscious of the cloud that had taken "all away". That is a very substantial change to take place in three years, but what else could we expect? The Chancellor of the Exchequer, after all, has been in charge of the till in the 'Old Curiosity Shop' for some time past now, and the shareholders clearly are bidden to expect 'Hard Times'. No wonder the Benches opposite two days ago presented the aspect of a depressed area. Indeed, if hon. Members opposite will forgive me for saying so, they looked to me for all the world like a congregation of undertakers' mutes."[16]

If Jones sometimes felt restrained from criticising the government's economic policy on the floor of the commons, he felt no compunction in highlighting the actions of the owners of a local colliery. In 1933, the SWMF was embroiled in a bitter dispute with mine owners over the attempts which were being made to replace the 'Fed' as the recognised trade union with the South Wales

Miners' Industrial Union, a company or 'scab' union. The biggest flashpoints in this dispute were at the Taff Merthyr Colliery and the Navigation Colliery in Bedwas, in the lower Rhymney Valley.[17]

Although he did not represent Bedwas (it was part of the Bedwellty division), many of his constituents worked in the colliery and, during an Adjournment Debate, he explained to MPs that he knew the area well:

"I was born in this valley. I lived in it all my life until the last few years. I know something of the history of Bedwas. I recall it as a very small village. My own relatives on my grandfather's side came from this very village and I have been acquainted with it from my youth upwards. It has grown from a small isolated village into a comparatively big modern mining township. There is only one colliery there and upon the colliery everybody in the village depends. There is practically no other means of livelihood available. When this colliery was started thousands of people gravitated towards it, habitations grew up around it, and, indeed, the colliery proprietors built a certain number of houses there so as to make it possible for more people to live in the neighbourhood."[18]

After setting the scene, he went on to coolly point out the inequity of the situation:

"Let Hon. Members on all sides try to visualise this situation. Here are thousands of people who have come from various parts of south Wales to earn their livelihood in this place. An edict goes forth from the colliery company that these thousands of people who have come there at the behest of that company and to work that company's colliery, are no longer to be employed there...I do not want to import into this matter any more feeling than there is in it already, but I know of thousands of people on my side of the valley who have been moved by this incident as I have never known them to be moved before."[19]

Shortly before the commons debate, a significant disturbance had occurred in Bedwas – referred to as a 'riot' – when police had charged a crowd assembled outside the local police station. Feeling that an attempt was going to be made to release two women who had earlier been arrested for assaulting a 'blackleg', the police called a local magistrate who read the Riot Act and the police charged the demonstrators. A number of people were injured and the police made numerous arrests, including four women, as Jones explained to MPs:

"I saw one of the women concerned in this case being taken under escort from Cardiff to the trial. I felt a sense of revulsion at seeing an obviously decent citizen

A Bedwas miner is welcomed home after the successful end of the 'Stay Down' strike in 1936. (Courtesy of National Museum Wales)

like that woman being taken away on such a comparatively flimsy charge to stand a trial and ultimately to be sent to prison."[20]

After a long and bitter struggle, the dispute came to an end in 1936 after the Fed organised a 'Stay Down' strike, which ended in victory for the Fed and the SWMF being recognised as the sole union at the colliery.

Although Morgan Jones never subscribed to the view that private enterprise was anathema to the creation of a more planned economy, he was strongly in favour of the introduction of public ownership in key industries, particularly the coal industry. He believed that nationalisation of the mines would enable the workers in that industry to exercise their ability for the good of their industry and the people of Britain. Accordingly, in February 1938, he gave his support to a private member's bill and spoke of the miners in glowing terms:

> *"…that there is no group of people in this country as politically advanced as the miners. They, too, have their sense of initiative. They, too, want to get away from being mere automata. There is no provision under the present system whereby the sense of initiative of the workers is utilised. In this bill the worker is invited to take his share in the actual task of governing the industry".*[21]

While Jones recognised that this bill was unlikely to progress far, he nevertheless concluded his case for public ownership by stating that:

> *"We shall be beaten today in the Lobby, I have no doubt, by people who, for one reason or another, have not even heard the arguments brought forward, but let the house not forget that we shall return with this bill year after year,*

in parliament after parliament, until at long last this industry is owned and controlled by the people and run in the interests of the nation at large."[22]

Throughout his life Morgan Jones was a patriotic Welshman. He spoke Welsh fluently and upheld the 'language of Heaven' whenever he could. For example, in May 1923, at the Eisteddfod organised by the National Union of Welsh Societies in Mountain Ash, he was influential in ensuring that the Welsh language's prominence was maintained and that English was proscribed from the festival's activities.[23]

He regularly attended the National Eisteddfod and, from time to time, made reference to things distinctly Welsh in his parliamentary speeches. In the 1936 Budget debate, for instance, he compared the "oppressive silence" on the government benches to an occasion at the National Eisteddfod when the bards were expected to cheer a distinguished visitor but did nothing. He recalled how the Eisteddfodic silence was broken when an instruction was shouted out, in Welsh, "Cheer, you devils". Jones said he felt like giving a similar helping hand to the government.[24]

Jones always believed that Wales ought to have a devolved and distinctive system of self-government, such as when, in his election address of 1922, he stated clearly that he supported self-government for Wales. Welsh needs ought to be addressed, he argued, in an appropriate and distinctive way. That did not mean, however, that the MP for Caerphilly had any time for the newly established Welsh nationalist party, Plaid Genedlaethol Cymru, now known as Plaid Cymru. It was Jones' view that socialism and nationalism were incompatible.

As we have seen, he initiated moves towards a Welsh national educational structure when a junior minister in the 1924 Labour government, and when a Welsh group of the PLP was formed in 1922 Morgan Jones became its first secretary. He later became chairman of the Welsh parliamentary party and when the all-party group sent a deputation to meet the prime minister Neville Chamberlain, in June 1938, to put the case for a secretary of state for Wales, Jones was asked to lead the delegation.[25] The arguments which were put to Neville Chamberlain, however, did not impress the prime minister and the idea was firmly rejected in a letter Jones received from Neville Chamberlain explaining why he did not accept the delegation's case:

'Dear Morgan Jones,
I send you this letter in fulfilment of my promise to the deputation from the Welsh Parliamentary Labour Party which I received at the House of Commons on the 30th June. As you will remember, I undertook to consider the arguments advanced on that occasion in support of the establishment of a Welsh Office, with a separate

Secretary of State for Wales, and to communicate my decision in due course. I have had an opportunity of thinking the matter over and I can now give you my considered reply.

Let me say at once that I am not lacking in sympathy for the argument from national sentiment which was presented by yourself and others, and that I recognise the existence in certain quarters of a feeling that the administration of Welsh affairs should, as far as may be possible, be concentrated in a single department. But it is my duty, in considering the matter, to have regard also to the practical considerations, and after examination of all the governing factors I have reached the conclusion that the request is not one that can be sustained.

Under the present system, while Welsh affairs are dealt with in the appropriate government offices in London, arrangements have been made – where this is possible – for their concentration in a separate division; and there are, of course, offices in Wales itself which handle individual questions, of a nature to be dealt with locally. To this extent, therefore, Wales is receiving the special treatment which was one of the objects of the deputation. I am satisfied of the efficiency of these arrangements, and I do not consider that Wales would receive any practical advantage from co-ordination of the various activities in a single department.

Such co-ordination would, moreover, involve considerable expenses in the establishment of a new office, the provision of staff, etc., and I do not feel, particularly at the present time when the calls on the Exchequer are many and heavy, that parliament could justly be asked to vote money for it.

The analogy of Scotland has been advanced not only by the deputation but on other occasions. I think, however, that it must be recognised that the two cases are not parallel. For Scotland has always had different systems of law and administration from those in force in England; indeed, even before the institution of the Scottish Office, most the Scottish administrative work was performed in Scotland and the Lord Advocate was, for all practical purposes, the head of a distinct Scottish Department in London. Wales, on the other hand, since Henry VIII's Act of 1535, has been closely incorporated with England and there has not been, and is not now, any distinct law and administrative system calling for the attention of a separate minister

In these circumstances while I fully appreciate the motive which led the members of the deputation to approach me, I fear that I must ask you to inform them that I do not feel able to comply with the request which they made when we met.

Yours sincerely,
(Signed) N. Chamberlain '[26]

Despite being rejected by Chamberlain, this was the start of a long campaign which was ultimately successful and culminated with the appointment of James Griffiths as the first secretary of state for Wales in 1964. Morgan Jones

Dyffryn House, a few miles west of Cardiff. (Courtesy of Jayne David)

deserves, perhaps, some of the credit for initiating that campaign and for foreshadowing Welsh devolution itself.

There was also another Welsh issue which Morgan Jones felt strongly about during the 1930s – the future of Dyffryn House in the Vale of Glamorgan. Dyffryn House was built by, and for many years was the home of the Cory family, one of the principal coal owning families of south Wales. The house itself was built by John Cory, while the extremely impressive Edwardian garden was the inspiration of his son. In the early 1930s, the house and its gardens were sold to Sir Cennydd Traherne, who later became Lord Lieutenant of Glamorgan. Maintaining the house and its gardens was an onerous burden for Sir Cennydd, and Jones was instrumental in persuading Sir Cennydd to pass ownership of the house and its gardens to Glamorgan County Council.[27] Today, following significant public investment, the house and its beautiful gardens are in the hands of the National Trust.[28]

Amongst his other interests in Wales, Jones also served on the Court of the University of Wales[29] and, at a more local level, he was a strong supporter of the Caerphilly District Miners' Hospital, which had been financed by local miners making weekly contributions from their wages.[30] The hospital was officially opened in 1923 and, in June 1930, Jones had the privilege of opening a new block, increasing the number of beds to 28 thus allowing admissions to be extended to the wives and families of the contributing colliers. The principle behind, and the operation of, the Miners' Hospital in Caerphilly was similar, in many ways, to that of the medical provision in Tredegar which inspired Aneurin Bevan to establish the National Health Service and, in 1948, Caerphilly Miners' Hospital became part of the NHS.[31]

Notes

1. F.W.S. Craig, *British Parliamentary Election Results: 1885-1975*, (Macmillan, 1976).
2. N. Thomas-Symonds, *Attlee – A Life in Politics*, (I.B. Tauris, 2010), p.62.
3. *Manchester Guardian*, April 24th, 1939.
4. Chris Williams, *Oxford Dictionary of National Biography*, op. cit.
5. *Holding Government to Account – 150 years of the Committee of Public Accounts*, (House of Commons, 2012).
6. *South Wales Argus*, April 24th, 1939.
7. *Holding Government to Account*, op. cit., p.18.
8. Ibid.
9. Ibid.
10. *Caerphilly Journal*, Feb 27th, 1932.
11. See, The National Industrial Development Council of Wales and Monmouthshire, *Second Industrial Survey of South Wales*, Vols. I, II, & III, (University of Wales Press, 1937).
12. Glyndwr G. Jones. *Cronicl Caerffili: A collection of notes relating to Caerphilly's past*, (self-published, 1973), p.22.
13. *Hansard*, July 22nd, 1936, col.586.
14. Ibid., col.587.
15. Ibid., col.589.
16. *Hansard*, April 6th, 1935, col.1702.
17. See, Wayne David, *Remaining True – A Biography of Ness Edwards*, op. cit., pp.12-39. Also, Hywel Francis and David Smith, *The Fed – a History of the South Wales Miners in the 20th Century*, op. cit., pp.113-144.
18. *Hansard*, July 18th, 1933, col.1757.
19. Ibid., col.1758.
20. Ibid., col.1759.
21. *Hansard*, February 4th, 1938, cols.633-634.
22. Ibid., cols.634-635.
23. Referred to by, Marie A. Williams and Geraint H. Jenkins, *Let's Do Our Best for the Ancient Tongue: the Welsh Language in the Twentieth Century*, (University of Wales Press, 2000), p.255.
24. *Hansard*, April 23rd, 1936, col.341.
25. Jim Griffiths, *Pages from Memory*, (J.M. Dent, 1969), pp.157-8.
26. Ibid.
27. *Merthyr Express*, April 29th, 1939.
28. *The History of Dyffryn House and Gardens*, (Glamorgan County Council, 1971), pp.5-6.
29. Entry in *Who Was Who Vol. III (1929-1940)*, (Bloomsbury, 2014).
30. Dennis G. Selwood, *Caerphilly Miners' District Hospital 1923-1948*, (self-published, 2012), p.50.
31. *Caerphilly Journal*, June 14th, 1930.

6

The Internationalist

Throughout his political life, Morgan Jones was a passionate internationalist. In fact, internationalism was absolutely central to his philosophy of socialism and, like many of his generation on the left who had lived through the First World War, he was determined to do everything possible to prevent the world slipping back into another global conflict.

Until the early 1930s, there was a high degree of unity in the Labour Party on foreign policy issues. Most agreed that the twin objectives of world peace and socialism could be successfully advanced through wholehearted support for the League of Nations and by general disarmament and opposition to militarism.

Morgan Jones gave a clear exposition of his views on peace and disarmament at an Inter-Parliamentary Union (IPU) conference in Geneva in 1932 and, although this was his first IPU conference, he delivered two long and significant speeches. The message he conveyed in both speeches was clear and resolute.

Following on from the conclusions of the world disarmament conference, also held in Geneva, Jones said that after six months of discussion it was not making anything like sufficient progress; there were, he said, to audible support from the conference, too many who wanted to make "mutual killing of each other a specially gentlemanly operation".[1] In some detail, he focussed on how the policy of reparations against Germany needed to be re-examined, telling the conference that, in his view, the issue of reparations, and the repayment of Europe's war debts to the United States, were being approached "too much in the spirit of war and not enough in the spirit of peace, too much in the spirit of revenge and too little in the spirit of reconciliation".[2]

On the subjects of "bombardment from the air" and "chemical warfare", Jones lamented the fact that there had not been agreement on prohibition and he expressed his "profound disappointment" that his own country had not taken a stronger lead.[3] The MP for Caerphilly also spoke out against what he called "the new spirit of economic nationalism", which was spreading throughout the world. For the best part of a century, he pointed out, Britain had upheld the principle of free trade, but had now succumbed to protectionism. Furthermore, the idea of protectionism was now being extended to the British Empire, with the result that a vast part of the world was being "roped in" under what Jones called "economic imperialism".[4]

His first speech to the IPU conference concluded with a powerful point that the "embitterments" which now existed were losing the youth of Europe; young people were beginning to say that "parliaments are no good" and instead they were turning towards dictatorship or revolution. Apocalyptically, Jones concluded by saying that the end result of this loss of trust and confidence in parliamentary democracy could mean that "our civilisation may be mutually engulfed in ruin". These words drew 'loud applause' from the IPU conference and, sadly, were to be only too accurate a prediction as the decade unfolded.[5]

The IPU conference proceeded to pass resolutions calling for a significant reduction of world armaments, cuts in military spending, the introduction of periodic and automatic weapons control, and strict limits on the manufacture and trade of arms.[6] All of this was unacceptable to the fascist delegation from Italy and in an indication of what the future held, they indignantly walked out of the conference.[7]

Even though Jones had onerous responsibilities as chair of the Public Accounts Committee and as Labour's shadow education spokesman, he also spoke from the frontbench on many foreign policy issues. In the early 1930s, when Japan invaded Manchuria and established a puppet regime

Morgan Jones at his ministerial desk during the 1930s. (Courtesy of Nick Sheaff)

there, Jones was given the responsibility of leading for the opposition. From the frontbench, he argued strongly that the British government ought to have been more proactive in trying to stiffen the resolve of the League of Nations to prevent Japan taking the action it did.[8]

In November 1933, in a debate on disarmament, Jones moved a motion on behalf of the opposition in the form of a vote of censure. The motion urged the government to adopt a comprehensive agreement for disarmament and then to present it to the disarmament conference. In a long speech, he presented a withering critique of the government's foreign policy.

However, when Jones moved on to the situation in the Far East and referred to Japan and its exit from the League of Nations, he lost his surefootedness. In an uncustomary lack of judgement, he made an accusation which he was made to justify.[9]

In the middle of his speech, he unwisely suggested that Conservative MPs had deliberately encouraged Japan to leave the League of Nations. There was uproar in the chamber and Jones was asked to give the names of those to whom he was referring. He conceded that he was unable to give "actual quotations", but insisted that Sir Austen Chamberlain, the MP for West Birmingham and a former Foreign Secretary, was one of those whose comments he could recall.[10]

Austen Chamberlain responded by saying emphatically that there was not "the slightest foundation" for this accusation, but Morgan Jones was adamant that he was "not going to withdraw a single word".[11]

Jones then went on to say "that strong and important Powers could do what they would, without expecting any violent action on the part of the League of Nations against them". The words "any violent action" were seized on by the prime minister, Ramsay MacDonald in his response. MacDonald, who still saw himself as a pacifist, wanted to know "what sort of violent action" Jones had in mind, and whether he had said this as part of "an official pronouncement from the opposition".[12]

Ramsay MacDonald had put his finger on an extremely important point. The leader of the Labour Party, George Lansbury, would have most definitely disagreed with Morgan Jones, but there was a growing body of opinion in the Labour Party who were now coming to hold Jones' point of view.

The following day was difficult for Jones. He made a personal statement in the House of Commons withdrawing his remarks saying that he had consulted *Hansard* – the official parliamentary record – and now realised that "under pressure" he had done Sir Austen "a grievous injustice". His apology was graciously accepted by Sir Austen.[13]

It has been suggested that Jones' *faux pas* referring to Sir Austen occurred because he was worried about the illness afflicting one of his daughters.[14] That may well have been the case and as far as parliament was concerned that was the end of the matter, but the story was taken up by the *Western Mail*. Mischievously, rather than simply reporting Jones' accusation and his subsequent apology, the paper embellished the events into an extensive satirical article.[15]

Although the piece was largely fabricated, it purported to be based on Morgan Jones' own words. In many respects the piece was misleading, but on the other hand some of it was not implausible and perhaps based on more than a grain of truth. The piece was also very amusing, even if it was at Jones' expense.

The article was entitled 'Morgan Jones' Humiliations and Ambitions' and it began with the author seemingly telling the reader how he bumped into Jones in the St. Stephen's entrance to parliament, just before the censure debate. We are told how Jones greets the journalist, informing him that he was the first Welshman ever to be chosen to move a censure motion on a government from the opposition frontbench. Jones then states that he is therefore certain to join the cabinet once Labour wins power, although his real ambition, it was suggested, was to become speaker of the commons. The attraction of this job was not only the good salary and other perks, there was also the likelihood of being elevated eventually to the House of Lords and becoming Viscount Caerphilly. Moreover, he planned to have Caerphilly cheese on his heraldic crest![16]

As to the forthcoming censure debate, the Caerphilly MP is supposed to have said that he had 'selected' Austen Chamberlain as his target because Chamberlain had a reputation of 'turning both cheeks' and, therefore, presumably he would be able to get away with his attack. The article concludes by referring to an alleged conversation the following day with a very chastened Morgan Jones. According to the journalist, Jones recalled what happened in the chamber saying that even the prime minister had risen to his feet and 'in a tone of withering contemptuousness' asked whether Morgan had the 'audacity' to make such a serious statement without being able to back it up.[17]

This parliamentary *faux pas* and his subsequent ridiculing in the *Western Mail* was undoubtedly discomforting and very embarrassing for Jones, yet he was determined not to let the matter lie and instead brought a libel action against the newspaper. A year after the offending article appeared, the case went to court and, after a light-hearted session, the judge gave a summing-up which was favourable to Jones. According to the judge, it was wrong for an individual to be libelled in this way, even if the piece was written largely in jest. The jury returned and declared in favour of Morgan Jones. He was awarded damages of £100; a not inconsiderable amount.[18]

This was a tumultuous time in international affairs. Not only had Japan invaded Manchuria, but in 1933 Hitler secured power in Germany and began a process of rearmament, withdrawing Germany from the League of Nations and the world disarmament conference, which collapsed soon after. This led to many inside the Labour Party, including the MP for Caerphilly, to question the strict pacifism which had inspired Labour's foreign policy throughout the 1920s.

Morgan Jones had referred to "violent action" by the League of Nations in his November 1933 commons speech – which featured in the court case – probably as a result of departing from his speaking notes, but he was certainly articulating the developing thinking of many on Labour's frontbench. Hugh Dalton soon emerged as one of the most prominent of those who was now openly questioning Labour's view that the use of force was always morally wrong and could never be justified. By the summer of 1934, the Labour Party's NEC and the PLP had accepted Arthur Henderson and Morgan Jones' view that there ought to be support for the collective peace-keeping machinery of the League and this became party policy at the Labour autumn conference of that year.[19]

The policy contained in the agreed statement, *For Socialism and Peace* did not, however, have the support of George Lansbury, the Labour leader. Lansbury had been ill when the policy was being written, and shortly before the conference at which it was adopted, Lansbury had made known his opposition.[20]

Soon after the party conference Mussolini's Italy invaded Abyssinia. The TUC General Council, the NEC of the Labour Party, and the PLP agreed a joint declaration condemning the Italian aggression and supporting any action by the League of Nations to enforce peace. At the Labour conference of 1935 in Brighton, it upheld that position after the leader of the Transport and General Workers' Union, Ernest Bevin, made an angry attack on George Lansbury and his pacifism, which precipitated Lansbury's resignation as Labour leader.[21]

Not long after the conference, Lansbury spoke in parliament reaffirming his absolute belief in pacifism yet, on the following day in a debate on the prorogation and dissolution of parliament before the general election which the government had called, Morgan Jones made an important and moving statement about his own personal beliefs.[22]

After paying tribute to George Lansbury for expressing the pacifist case with "eloquence and courage",[23] he went on to explain in some detail how and why the League of Nations should play the central role in collective global security. If the current aggressor, Italy, was allowed to "violate" the undertakings that had been made, said Jones, then "none of us would look to the League in future to give us any protection against aggression directed against ourselves". It was therefore necessary to ensure that the Covenant of the League was adhered to in its entirety.

The plaque, at the Caerphilly Visitors' Centre, that commemorates the volunteers of the International Brigade who fought fascism in Spain.

The criticism Jones levelled at the government was that it did not rest its authority "upon the collective forces available to all nations, but upon the individual measure of force at the disposal of a particular nation".[24] The Caerphilly MP argued that the government only paid lip service to the League of Nations because it did not accept that the League should provide "collectively" the security for "any aggrieved nation", and it followed that it was the duty of individual nations to make the League "powerful enough to deal with any aggressor".[25]

Morgan Jones had therefore moved away from the strict pacifist position he had held during the First World War and during the 1920s. Now Labour, under its new leader Clem Attlee, adopted foreign policy positions, supported by Jones, which allowed the party to respond more effectively to the changing international situation. Differences in the party over defence and foreign policy continued, however, and Labour, despite its move away from pacifism, maintained its opposition to the government's expenditure on arms by opposing the annual arms estimates.

Like many on the Left, Jones continued to have faith in the possibility of strengthening the League of Nations and making it an effective international institution. The attack upon democracy and the civil war that followed in Spain contributed to the development of his view of the need to vigorously defend democracy.

In July 1936, within 10 days of the fascist rising in Spain, Jones pointed out to the House of Commons that the democratically elected government of the Spanish people was being directly challenged by fascists.[26] When interrupted by a Conservative MP who said indignantly that the communists were supporting the Republican government, Jones retorted that this should be welcomed and was in contrast to the attitude of sections of the right-wing press in Britain which had "scarcely been able to conceal their desire to see democracy beaten, finally, in Spain".[27]

Later in 1936, there was a suggestion that the British government would seek to prevent volunteers from Britain joining the International Brigade to support the Republican cause. Jones made it clear that Labour would oppose any ban unless it was "applied all round and accepted by all nations".[28] He also urged the government to provide medical supplies to hospitals in "Madrid and elsewhere".[29] There had been a delegation of MPs to Spain and they had returned with graphic descriptions of how bad the situation was.

Jones was under no misapprehension about how communism, as well as fascism, was creating instability and conflict in Europe. In a forlorn tone he asked rhetorically "Why cannot the leaders of all nations – I say 'all nations', without exception – accept the simple proposition that the internal affairs of a country are its own?"[30]

Clearly, Jones felt passionately about what was happening in Spain and he expressed the horror felt by many, when he said Spain had slid back into the "barbarism of the Middle Ages" and he sincerely hoped that the British government would do all it could to bring an end to the conflict.[31] Though he warned the government that it would be quite wrong if General Franco were granted "belligerent rights" because, as Jones said, Franco was in rebellion against his own government and as such he should be regarded as the aggressor.[32]

By the end of 1936, Labour had strengthened its position in support of the Republican government and, in February 1938, Jones initiated a two-hour debate in the commons on the Nazis' bombing of the Basque city of Guernica.[33] Some months after the attack on a defenceless civilian population, it was becoming clear that many hundreds and possibly well over a thousand civilians had lost their lives in what was the first mass bombing by Nazi Germany's Luftwaffe.

Jones opened the debate by arguing against aerial bombardment in general.[34] He referred to how there was a strong feeling in the disarmament conference that air armaments should be outlawed, and that the General Commission of the conference had agreed that "air attack against the civilian population should be absolutely prohibited".[35] He then moved on from his general comments about aerial disarmament to specific remarks about what was happening in Spain.[36]

Shortly before the debate, Philip Noel-Baker, the Labour MP for Derby, had lent Jones a copy of George Steer's recently published, incisive and moving book *The Tree of Gernika: a Field Study of Modern War*.[37] Steer was a journalist with *The Times* and had witnessed at first hand the atrocities in the Basque city. Jones quoted from the book to good effect, prefacing the selected extract by saying, "At the risk of harrowing the feelings of Honourable Members", before quoting the following passage from Steer's book:

"An escort of Heinkel 51's, the same perhaps that had molested us that afternoon, were waiting for this moment. 'Till now they had been machine-gunning the roads round Gernika, scattering, killing or wounding sheep and shepherds. As the terrified population streamed out of the town they dived low to drill them with their guns. Women were killed here whose bodies I afterwards saw. It was the same technique as that used at Durango on 31ˢᵗ March, nearly a month back."[38]

Following the speech Noel-Baker wrote enthusiastically to Steer, telling him that his book was 'quite brilliant' and remarking that Jones had quoted it 'sensibly'. He did also add that Jones' speech 'sounded better than it reads'.[39]

Jones admitted that his proposed motion did not go nearly as far as he or Labour had wanted. However, as he said in his closing remarks, he was keen for other countries to follow the British example, and for this to happen it was necessary for it to command the support of the government as well as the opposition.[40] The motion was therefore essentially broad and consensual. It read as follows:

'That in the opinion of this house, the growing horror of aerial bombardment of defenceless civilians should be expressed in an international agreement to co-operate in its prohibition, and urges his Majesty's Government to exert its influence to this end.'[41]

With the support of Anthony Eden, the foreign secretary, the motion was carried.

At the same time, Jones realised that if Franco was successful in Spain it would have huge implications for Britain and indeed the world. Victory for Franco would, he said in July 1938, give "a tremendous impetus to the fascist movement in Europe" and create "enormous complications" for France who would have a potentially hostile neighbour on its Pyrenean border.[42]

The Spanish Civil War had a profound impact on Jones' political views and it took him still further from his earlier uncompromising pacifist views. If the Spanish Civil War had an impact on Jones, so did the rise of the Nazi Party in Germany, in particular their treatment of Jews. Jones had developed strong links with the Jewish community, not least because in the 1930s he and his family were living in Golders Green where there was a large Jewish population, and due to his numerous visits to the United States where he had gained a wider respect for the Jewish people.[43]

As reports of the appalling treatment of the Jewish community in Nazi Germany began to appear, Jones became increasingly concerned. In a 'supply debate' on foreign affairs in July 1938, before the Sudetenland had been ceded to Germany, he suggested that if the Germans had shown more "humanity" towards the Jews in Germany, especially children, then their alleged concern about German speakers in the Sudetenland might be taken more seriously.[44] This was one of Morgan Jones' last contributions in the House of Commons and he commented that his wife "would not sleep easily" if she knew, as he did, the "desperate situation" of the Jews.[45]

With the clouds of international conflict gathering across the world, in the spring of 1938 Jones wrote an article in *Labour*, a discussion broadsheet of the Labour movement. Entitled 'Perplexities of a Pacifist',[46] his 1,000-word article calmly and rationally considered how pacifists in the Great War, like himself, ought to respond to the grave international situation.

He began by reaffirming his opposition to war; it was, he said, a 'bestial, bloody business', and the case against war 'be it from the political, economic, moral, or Christian point of view remains inviolate and inviolable'. Jones added, however, that there were 'difficulties which many pacifists in the last war are feeling keenly'.[47] Undoubtedly, he placed himself in this category. There was, he argued, an alternative to war and it was an approach based on discussion, argument and arbitration, and 'given the will, there must be a way' to prevent a 'conflagration' which could lead to 'the destruction of civilisation'.[48]

Reaffirming his view that there needed to be a 'machinery' in place for 'the just resolution of international disputes', Jones argued this was precisely why the League of Nations was established. While he accepted that the League had weaknesses, faults and 'manifest shortcomings', it nevertheless provided the means by which disputes could be settled peacefully between nations.[49]

He did, however, recognise that there was a profound problem in that many of the 'Covenants, pacts [and] agreements' had not been observed. If words were enough then there would have been no invasion of Manchuria and China, and no war in Abyssinia and Spain. Jones stated that:

"Pledges are solemnly given, treaties signed and sealed. Promises have actually been given one day, only to be broken on the next. The word of some statesmen is quite worthless. They break faith. They do not honour their bond…as a consequence nations which have traditions which they value, institutions which they cherish, ideals which they hold inseparably associated with the cause of democracy and of freedom, tremble with fear and apprehension for the future".[50]

In a clear reference to the Axis powers, Jones identified the problem: the nations of the world were being faced by 'gangsters' intent on destroying the machinery of the League of Nations so that they 'might proceed unchallenged'.[51]

His answer was that it was necessary for pacifists to be in favour of creating a 'collective security' to defend the international rule of law and its global instituion.[52]

In other words, like the Labour Party as a whole, Jones was advocating that the League of Nations should be the means of providing 'collective' defence and security for the law-abiding nations of the world. This may have been a long way from the unqualified pacifism which Morgan Jones espoused during the Great War and throughout the 1920s, but it was a rational, intellectually sustainable and principled response to the aggression which was now in evidence across the world.

Throughout his life, Jones was passionately concerned about international affairs and always sought to uphold the self-determination of all peoples. The future of India was the most contentious colonial issue of the day and, as such, India was often at the top of his international agenda.

During the 1920s, Britain's hold over India gradually weakened as the Congress Party of Gandhi and Nehru became more strident in its opposition to British rule and sympathisers in Britain began to organise as well. Even before Jones was elected to parliament, he supported the British auxiliary to the India Home Rule League.[53]

In 1929, the British Viceroy of India announced that dominion status was now the somewhat vague aim of British foreign policy, but his position failed to satisfy the increasingly assertive Indian Congress Party. January 1930 saw the Congress (as the Congress Party was known) commit itself to nothing less than Indian independence and Gandhi began his campaign of

WHITHER INDIA?

By

MORGAN JONES, M.P.

ONE PENNY

Published by

THE LABOUR PARTY

Jones' 1934 publication on the future of India.

civil disobedience, which was suspended the following year in return for the release of political prisoners.

Little real progress was made at discussions between Congress leaders and the British government in London in the autumn of 1931, and even though Morgan Jones spoke for many when he said in the House of Commons that he hoped some agreed position could somehow be reached and the "good will of the Indian people" would be secured,[54] Gandhi returned to India to resume non-cooperation.

Another fruitless round-table conference was held before the government set up the Joint Select Committee on Indian Constitutional Reform. This committee was made up of nearly 30 senior members of both houses of parliament; the commons' representatives included R.A. Butler, Sir Austen Chamberlain and Sir Samuel Hoare from the government side and Clem Attlee and Morgan Jones from the Labour Party.

The final report of the committee in fact consisted of three reports: the majority report, that of the so-called Salisbury Group and the minority Labour report. In a pamphlet printed by the Labour Party, with an introduction by its leader, George Lansbury, Jones set out why Labour believed the majority report was insufficiently radical in its approach.[55]

In some detail, he explained how the majority report failed to map out the kind of approach that was clearly needed. The Labour members thought that the proposed 'Autonomy for the Indian Provinces' was far too limited, with inadequate proposals to extend the franchise.[56] They also believed that the plan for a federal legislature was inadequate, especially the proposal to place foreign policy in the hands of the Governor-General, rather than with the Federal government.[57] The pamphlet also explained why the Labour MPs believed the recommendations to limit democratic economic governance and protect British commercial interests were unjustified.[58]

In short, the Caerphilly MP explained that the Labour Party believed that the majority report was 'much too conservative in outlook'. It was, he said, 'reactionary both economically and politically', and overlooked 'the fundamental claim of the Indian people to determine their own line of development'. Jones thought that, at the very least, the Indian people ought to have equality of status with the dominions, so that there could be real movement towards self-determination and self-government.[59]

The work of the Joint Select Committee proved to be the most significant initiative on India during the 1930s and its recommendations formed the basis of the 1935 India Act. In essence, the Act formulated a federal structure for India, and Jones made a significant contribution to the debates in parliament. One of his most telling speeches was on a clause which would disqualify a person with a prison conviction from standing for election to the Indian parliament. Perhaps thinking of his own time as a conscientious objector, the Member for Caerphilly told his fellow MPs:

> *"Let us remember that there are undoubtedly tens of thousands who participated in the civil disobedience campaign in India who will be affected by this clause and precluded from election to parliament. Who are these people? They are, in the main, young Indians. They are young people who might have been misguided but who believed very intensely that they were, according to their rights, serving their country. I know that the law can say today that this shall be done and that shall not be done, but there comes a time when individual citizens of the state have to determine for themselves whether they ought even to obey the law."*[60]

The clause was passed by parliament, as was the bill as a whole, but following opposition from the rulers of the Princely States as well as the Congress, the blueprint was never fully introduced. The Congress was strongly in favour of nothing less than full independence, which it achieved after the Second World War, from a Labour Government.

The other foreign policy that consumed much of Morgan Jones' time was Palestine. From his earliest days in parliament, he had been sympathetic to the case for a Jewish homeland in Palestine and in 1922, soon after he was elected, he made a speech about the future of Palestine in which he concluded:

> *"…the return of the Jewish people to Palestine—this is the pith of my argument—is well grounded in history and tradition. These people have looked forward to this return to their national home for generations, if not for centuries. Their prophets, their priests, their singers—all have taught them to believe that at some dim and distant day they would return to their ancestral home".*[61]

Throughout the 1920s, Josiah Wedgewood, an ex-Liberal Labour MP, and Morgan Jones were the two MPs who took a consistent line of supporting independence for India while also making the case for a 'Jewish National Home'.[62] Although the contexts were very different, both Wedgewood and Jones believed that the principle of self-determination was appropriate to both situations.[63]

The Balfour Declaration of 1917 was broadly accepted by the Labour Party, and at the 1920 party conference it was unanimously agreed that there should be a Jewish settlement in Palestine with, crucially, equality between Arabs and Jews. This was Jones' view as well.[64] For most of the 1920s there were relatively few disturbances in Palestine, and Jewish immigration gradually increased. However, because of the growing persecution of the Jews in Europe, the rate of Jewish immigration rapidly increased during the 1930s. Conflict between Arabs and Jews became more widespread and, as tension in Palestine grew, the Labour Party established an advisory committee to draw up a long-term policy for Palestine. Morgan Jones was a member of that committee.[65]

In 1936, both the general council of the TUC and the Labour Party conference passed resolutions re-affirming support for a Jewish homeland and continued Jewish immigration. While the terrible living conditions of many Arabs was acknowledged, there was also a growing admiration of what was being achieved in Jewish *kibbutzim* in Palestine and an increasing awareness of the plight of Jews in Nazi Germany.

It was against this backdrop that Jones had to make some of his most diplomatically challenging parliamentary contributions. As in so much of his international work, his starting point was support for the League of Nations and their decisions, and he was an upholder of Britain's presence in Palestine because it was determined by a mandate of the League.[66] Proposals to divide Palestine into Jewish and Arab cantons, or later a formal partition, were not easy for Jones or indeed the Labour Party to support,[67] although this is precisely what the government's Royal Commission on Palestine proposed in July 1937.

This presented Labour with a dilemma. Clem Attlee, Labour's new leader, unlike Morgan Jones, had little real sympathy for Zionism and he was reluctant to support the demise of the mandate as an international agreement. Yet, under pressure from those, like Jones, who were more sympathetic to Jewish aspirations, he was mindful of the need to maintain the party's friendship with the Jewish community in Britain.[68] He also recognised that it would not be politically possible for Labour to oppose a plan which had the backing of both the British government and the Zionists.[69]

In the parliamentary debate on the Royal Commission's report (known as the Peel Commission), various Labour MPs put forward a number of arguments, often contradictory, concerning the Arabs and their leaders. A number of members condemned the reactionary and allegedly fascist views of the Arab national leadership and deplored the Arab gang terror. The assumption of many was that the Arab leaders did not speak for the Arab people as a whole. What was needed, one Labour MP said, was an arrangement for Arabs and Jews to live together and co-operate for their mutual advantage.[70]

It fell to Morgan Jones to perform a difficult balancing act when he spoke in the debate in the House of Commons. In a speech which was in many ways extremely circumspect, he declared that he supported continuing immigration of Jews to Palestine, but that he was not "pro-Arab or pro-Jew".[71] His crucial point was that he wanted parliament to discuss the issue of partition "much more fully than has yet been done before it takes its final decision and is committed to the matter".[72] Jones believed that the way the government and parliament had approached the India situation provided a useful example which could be followed in the case of Palestine. A careful approach was needed because "pledges and promises" had been made to both sides over the years and now this was causing "perplexity and confusion". Realising that the stakes were high, he worried that if "care" was not taken then there was the very real risk of conflict between "the Moslem world and Jewry".[73]

In terms of the detail of the report, Jones was concerned about the criticism of the British mandate in Palestine. For him, it was unfair for the report to attack the mandate when there had been real progress in the social and economic position of so many Arabs. It was also wrong that the report questioned the determination of the British to implement the Balfour Declaration and, even more reprehensible was the suggestion that the administration of justice and security showed "leniency" towards Arabs engaged in political agitation, even when "carried to the point of violence and murder".[74]

Morgan Jones argued that even if the case for partition was accepted, the specific proposals of the commission were "unthinkable and wholly unacceptable".[75] He explained in some detail why the partition of Palestine into a Jewish state, an Arab state and, what he called, a Mandatory state was poorly thought out. There were, he stressed, a whole range of problems that needed further debate and discussion. Amongst these were the administration of the port of Jaffa, where the commission had proposed a Joint Harbour Board, and the position of Jerusalem. The Peel Commission suggested that Jerusalem should continue to be held under British mandate, but Jones held the view that Jerusalem is "the heart and soul of the Jewish hope in respect of Palestine" and should be recognised as such.[76]

He concluded that the complexities and sensitivities of Palestine were such that everyone involved had to "walk with care and circumspection". Much more discussion was needed so that a scheme could be worked out that was acceptable to both Jews and Arabs.[77]

The debate on the Peel Report continued after Jones had left London for his work with the Royal Commission on the British West Indies, but the need for all parties to remember his wise words became ever more apparent.

Jones' last contribution on the position of the Jewish people came in an article in *Labour* in August 1938 – his last published article – and focussed on *The Problem of the Stateless Jew*.[78] He began his piece with a depressing description of the plight of the Jewish people in Nazi Germany:

> *'Since Hitler came to power in Germany, Jew baiting has almost been accepted as a national pastime. The government has declared its intention of ridding itself of Jews. But if a Jew wished to leave he was to be permitted to pay a "flight" tax of*

25 per cent of the value of his property, while the rest had to place to an account of [sic] "Speermarks" for which he would receive in exchange less than 10 per cent of its nominal value'.[79]

He also described 'the foul stream of barbarism' in Germany's neighbouring countries – Poland, Romania and Hungary. In Europe, Jones wrote, five million Jews were living in 'constant terror'. In such a situation, there was now a responsibility to give material expression to the 'outraged concern of Humanity'.[80] He welcomed the fact that President Roosevelt had convened a conference at Evian, in France, to consider what could be done to help Jewish refugees but, to date, Jones believed that the 'public utterances' from the conference had been 'not very impressive'.[81]

Morgan Jones believed that the conference had, however, achieved something: it had 'brought to the notice of the civilised world' the 'horrible problem of wanton cruelty on the one hand, and on the other undeserved suffering'. The conference was due to resume its work in the autumn and Jones was hopeful that the permanent committee which had been established would bring forward detailed information as to what could be done to provide 'refuge' for Jewish people.[82]

However, Jones also lamented the inaction of the British Government. In his view, Britain ought to have encouraged Jewish immigration to Palestine, it should have allowed settlement of Jewish people to take place in the British colonies, and refugees should have welcomed into Britain. It was up to us, he wrote, the 'democratic people of Britain' to:

'show that we recognise the problem as one which we must help to solve. We have an honourable tradition of which we may justly be proud. We have ever offered asylum to those who are hounded out of their own countries, and have sought peace among us. Let not that tradition be broken'.[83]

Notes

1. *Union Interparlementaire, Compte Rendu de la XXVIIIc Conférence, 20 au 26 Juillet 1932,* (Inter-Parliamentary Union Archives, House of Commons), p.480.
2. Ibid., p.303.
3. Ibid., p.304.
4. Ibid., p.305.
5. Ibid., p.306.
6. Yefim Zarjevski, *The People Have the Floor: A History of the Inter-Parliamentary Union,* (Dartmouth Publishing Co. Ltd., 1989), p.82.

7.   Ibid., pp.82-83.
8.   *Hansard*, November 13th, 1933, cols.579-584.
9.   Ibid., cols.579-593.
10. Ibid., col.582.
11. Ibid., col.583.
12. Ibid., col.594.
13. *Hansard*, November 14th, 1933, cols.739-740. See also R. Bassett, *Democracy and Foreign Policy. A case study: the Sino-Japanese Dispute, 1931-1933*, London School of Economic and Political Science, 1952, p.525.
14. *Western Mail*, November 15th, 1933.
15. *Western Mail*, November 16th, 1933.
16. Ibid.
17. Ibid.
18. *Western Mail*, October 17th, 1934.
19. Labour Party, annual conference report, 1934.
20. John Shepherd, *George Lansbury: At the Heart of Old Labour*, 2007, p.318.
21. See John Shepherd, op. cit., for a detailed exposition of the circumstances which led to Lansbury's resignation.
22. *Hansard*, October 23rd, 1935, cols.255-269.
23. Ibid., col.255.
24. Ibid., col.267.
25. Ibid.
26. *Hansard*, July 27th, 1936. col.1196.
27. Ibid., cols.1196-1197.
28. Ibid.
29. Ibid.
30. *Hansard*, December 18th, 1936, cols.2822-2823.
31. Ibid., col.2825.
32. Ibid., col.2826.
33. *Hansard*, February 2nd, 1938, col.305.
34. Ibid.
35. Ibid., col.307.
36. Ibid., cols.308-309.
37. Paul Preston, *We Saw Spain Die, The Sentimental Adventurer – Foreign Correspondents in the Spanish Civil War*, 2008, p.284.
38. *Hansard*, February 2nd, 1938, cols.308-309.
39. Quoted by Paul Preston, op. cit., p.284.
40. *Hansard*, February 2nd, 1938, col.310.
41. Ibid., col.305.
42. *Hansard*, July 26th, 1938, cols.2968 – 2969.
43. Recollections of Margaret Sheaff in conversation with Nick Sheaff, 2011.
44. *Hansard*, July 26th, 1938, col.2969.
45. Letter from Margaret Sheaff to Wayne David, October 23rd, 2012.
46. Morgan Jones, 'Perplexities of a Pacifist', *Labour*, August 1938. pp.158-159.
47. Ibid.
48. Ibid.
49. Ibid.
50. Ibid.

51. Ibid.
52. Ibid.
53. Shodhganga, Inflibnet Centre, *Activities of the Indian Home Rule Leagues in Britain (1916-1920)*, Chapter V of an anonymous PhD. thesis, pps.359-446.
54. *Hansard*, December 3rd, 1931, col.1335.
55. Morgan Jones, *Whither India*, (Labour Party, 1935).
56. Ibid.
57. Ibid.
58. Ibid.
59. Ibid.
60. *Hansard*, March 12th, 1935, col.274.
61. *Hansard*, July 4th, 1922, col.327.
62. Partha Sarathi Gupta, *The Zionist Lobby in the British Labour Party*, p.LII, Indian History Congress. Proceedings of the 36th Session, Aligarch, 1976.
63. Ibid.
64. See Preface, Joseph Gormy, *The British Labour Movement and Zionism 1917-1948*, 1983.
65. F.L. Lepkin, 'The British Labour Party and Zionism', (masters thesis), Simon Fraser University, 1966, p.49.
66. *Hansard*, July 21st, 1937, col.2256.
67. Joseph Gormy, op. cit., p.137.
68. Ibid.
69. *Hansard*, July 21st, 1937, Joseph Gormy, op. cit., p.139.
70. Ibid., cols.2246-2312.
71. Ibid., col.2253.
72. Ibid.
73. *Hansard*, July 21st, 1937, col.2264.
74. Ibid., col.2258.
75. Ibid., col.2259.
76. Ibid., col.2263.
77. Ibid., col.2264.
78. Morgan Jones, 'The Problem of the Stateless Jew', *Labour*, August 1938, pp.237-238.
79. Ibid.
80. Ibid.
81. Ibid.
82. Ibid.
83. Ibid.

7

The West Indies and the Last Year

The last issue which captured Morgan Jones' attention was the situation in the British West Indies. Here, in the 1930s, the government was facing an extremely serious situation.

Starting in British Honduras in 1934, there was huge labour unrest and rioting in virtually every British colony in the region. Jones felt strongly that Britain ought to be doing much more to address the root causes of the social disturbances. In a speech in the House of Commons in June 1938, he made his views clear, saying:

Riot in St. Kitts, 1935. (Courtesy of St. Kitts & Nevis Observer)

"there have been disturbances in Barbados, St. Lucia, Antigua, British Guiana, the Bahamas, St. Kitts, and now in Jamaica, all during the last three years…If agitators were responsible – I say "if" – they must have had very fruitful soil on which to work.

Anybody who has made even the most cursory study of conditions in the West Indies must have seen at once that the conditions are such as to make us all feel a sense of shame at the situation which now exists. It is a hundred years since we freed the slaves in Jamaica. The ancestors of many of these people were taken there unwillingly. We are responsible for their being there, and it is our business to see whether we cannot do something more than we have done to make their lives a little more bearable than they are. The right hon. Gentleman said that there are no people in the world who are more attached to Britain than are these people. I am inclined to think we have abused their loyalty. Perhaps they have taken too much on trust.

As I see them, the problems that have led to the recent disturbances are partly economic and partly constitutional…there are obvious economic grievances which must exercise the minds of these people, however illiterate they may be. Wages scarcely bear to be spoken about—they are disgraceful, and there is no other word to describe them ... The average rate of wages for labourers in government employ is: skilled or unskilled, 2s. 6d. to 3s. 6d. per day. Private employers pay skilled men from 3s. to 3s. 6d. per day, and unskilled men from 2s. to 2s. 6d. per day. Women in private employ get from 1s. 6d. to 1s. 8d. per day. I have in my possession a batch of press reports dealing with the situation in Jamaica. I have not seen one report from a press correspondent in which there is a suggestion that the wages are anything like that—if there was one, I may have overlooked it, and if so, I apologise. The quotations I have are taken from The Times, The Daily Telegraph and many other newspapers; and not one of them has mentioned any figures approaching the ones I have quoted. I do not understand this, but it is worth our while to find out what are the facts. I trust that we shall have that information available as soon as this commission, or some other commission, has reported on the matter. It is true that mechanisation enters into industry in Jamaica as elsewhere, and, therefore, the number of those employed must tend to be reduced. Still, those who are employed ought to be guaranteed a decent living wage. Unless they are guaranteed such a wage, the purchasing power, even of those who are at work, is limited, and to that degree the stability of the community is threatened."[1]

He then proceeded to describe the housing conditions of many in Jamaica, sourcing *The Times* and a series of what he called "remarkable articles" by the writer Harold Stannard. He said:

"In the issue of 25ᵗʰ May we read: The conception of a decent standard of life at once reflects itself in housing conditions. A lower middle-class man who lives in the new residential suburbs of Kingston, Jamaica, is, on the whole, better housed than a man of corresponding standing in London, but the gulf between his bungalow and the hovel in which the poor country labourer dwells is wider than that between the modern English housing estate and the slums which are now disappearing. The first time I saw one of these hovels I could hardly believe that it was intended for human occupation. Strands of dried bamboo are woven round a framework of stakes and the "room" thus formed is covered with palm thatch. There is no furniture except sacking on the earth and some sort of table to hold the oil-stove. To look from these huts to the neat little wooden bungalows by which the better employers are replacing them is to pass from barbarism to civilisation. Urban conditions are, if anything, worse. In a region of Kingston now marked down for slum clearance are shacks put together anyhow out of the sides of packing cases and sheets of corrugated iron. These shelters were evidently run up just after the earthquake. The shocking thing is that it has taken 30 years and special slum clearance legislation to get rid of them. No one could paint a more horrifying picture than that. It is a terrible indictment of the neglect, I will not say by this government, but by governments, of the housing situation in Jamaica."²

The consummate parliamentarian. (Courtesy of Nick Sheaff)

Relying on *The Times* again, Jones described the terrible social conditions in Kingston, Jamaica. The slum conditions were, he said, "horrifying".³ He then went on to ask his fellow MPs:

"How can we ask people to live contently under such conditions as those described in the quotation? Is there any ground for surprise at the recent disturbances? The

surprising thing is, not that such disturbances should have occurred, but that they should not have occurred long ago…The state of poverty among them [the population] is obviously appalling. Their food is very poor in quality…and the condition of sanitation is exceedingly bad."[4]

In August 1938, the government responded to the situation by appointing a Royal Commission to investigate the social and economic conditions in Britain's West Indies colonies and to make recommendations about how the situation could be improved. The commission was chaired by Walter Guinness, 1st Baron Moyne, and was henceforth known as the Moyne Commission. Other members of the commission included experts in agriculture, economics and social reform in the West Indies, and a former governor of Jamaica. There was also the distinguished trade unionist Sir Walter Citrine, general secretary of the TUC and the president of the International Federation of Trade Unionists, and providing the party political input and balance were Ralph Assherton, a Conservative MP, and Morgan Jones from Labour.[5]

Shortly after Prime Minister Neville Chamberlain signed the Munich Agreement with Hitler – which deeply dismayed Jones – the members of the commission sailed out together to the West Indies, in October 1938, on Baron Moyne's private motor yacht. They had plans to stay in the West Indies for six months and collect evidence in all the main British colonies, including Jamaica, Bermuda, the Windward Islands, Barbados, British Honduras, Trinidad and British Guiana.[6] On arriving in the West Indies in January, the commission immediately began work and attracted an enormous amount of media and public attention.

The commission's first port of call was Kingston, Jamaica, and the members were immediately appalled at the living and working conditions they found. Walter Citrine felt so strongly about what he had seen and heard that, independently of the other members of the commission, he quickly established links with the British Caribbean Worker's Movement and put his full personal support behind the fledging trade union movement. This caused huge tension within the commission and a number of the other members felt that Citrine's 'freelancing' might lead to further civil unrest.[7] Although Citrine's activities were well-received by many ordinary Jamaicans, there was real concern amongst the West Indian business community. As one Jamaican newspaper reported, 'Sir Walter Citrine is the sort of man whom you dislike violently or like ardently: there is no happy medium'.[8]

The other member of the commission who attracted a great deal of media attention was Morgan Jones. Undoubtedly, he was as shocked as Citrine, and everyone else on the commission, by the social conditions which they found and he worked with Citrine to give advice on how the workers might organise.

For example, F.A. Hoyes noted how, 'Sir Walter Citrine, general secretary of the British TUC, and Labour MP Morgan Jones gave the organisers of the league invaluable advice on how they should build up the political and industrial sections of the working class movement in Barbados".[9] However, unlike Citrine, Jones adopted a collegiate approach to the work of the commission. His lines of inquiry and his questioning were always forensic and hard hitting, but he never broke ranks with the other commission members and throughout he adopted a constructive approach to the commission's work.

His contribution was widely praised in the West Indies' press and the *Jamaican Daily Gleaner* went so far as to state that 'The outstanding and most charming personality amongst the Royal Commission is Mr Morgan Jones'.[10] Writing under the name of The Rediot, the correspondent went on to say that Jones 'possesses a very keen intellect and a rich sense of humour, which he uses with consummate skill in getting evidence for the Royal Commission'.[11]

The correspondent also described Jones as 'very affable' and reported on a talk he had given to the Readers and Writers Club of Jamaica.[12]

The journalist described how the Caerphilly MP 'spellbound' his audience by skilfully deploying his wit and extensive knowledge through a 'sonorous' voice.[13] Jones' talk was about the work of the commission, but he also gave a moving description of the island of Jamaica. "You have an island second to none in beauty", he said. "There is not a dull mile, so far as my experience goes, in the whole island. It is a gem set in a crystal sea". However, Jones also went on to say that Jamaica was "seared with many uglinesses, some uglinesses of a physical kind, some uglinesses of a moral kind, and these things

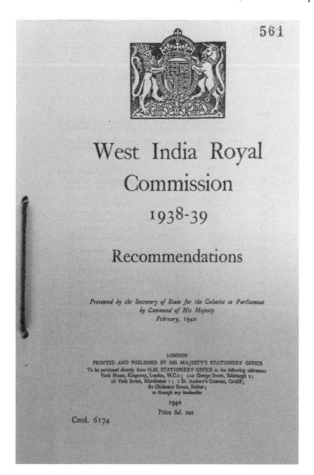

561

West India Royal Commission

1938-39

Recommendations

Presented by the Secretary of State for the Colonies to Parliament by Command of His Majesty February, 1940

LONDON
PRINTED AND PUBLISHED BY HIS MAJESTY'S STATIONERY OFFICE
To be purchased directly from H.M. STATIONERY OFFICE at the following addresses:
York House, Kingsway, London, W.C.2; 120 George Street, Edinburgh 2;
26 York Street, Manchester 1; 1 St. Andrew's Crescent, Cardiff;
80 Chichester Street, Belfast;
or through any bookseller
1940
Price 6d. net
Cmd. 6174

Front cover of the West Indies Royal Commission's recommendations, 1940.

are a challenge to the young people in the name of their country to help their country to rise above and clean out these horrible scars".[14] The key to improving the position of the island and its people was "education"; education not for self, but for the good of the "country". Jones concluded by stating that "education is one of the sharpest tools for cutting away the jungle of obstacles that lie in the path of the people of this island". His comments were extremely well received.[15]

From Jamaica, the commission divided into two. One group, led by the vice chairman, went to the Windward Islands and the other group, under the chairmanship of Baron Moyne, went to the Leeward Islands and British Honduras.[16] Morgan Jones was in the chairman's group and, following the visit to British Honduras, he wrote a comprehensive report about the education system in the colony and what, in his view, needed to change.[17]

Jones' view was that the education services in the country were 'woefully defective'.[18] He further stated that in the schools the class sizes were very large; the school buildings were unsuitable, with poor quality furniture; books were in short supply; and, most seriously, he found the teaching staff as a whole to be of poor quality, with many of the teachers having simply been retained after they had been pupils themselves at the schools.[19]

Most of the schools were run, Jones observed, by various Protestant religious denominations and all too frequently the teachers were 'appointed at least as much for their competence to do church work as to teach'. He noted, however, that the situation was much better with the Catholic schools.[20]

Jones also observed, with a great deal of concern, that the government permitted its educational system to be 'completely dominated by denominational considerations'. For the MP for Caerphilly, it was vital that the government immediately assumed responsibility for providing post-primary education for children, 'regardless of the convenience of denominational bodies'.

He also argued that there needed to be 'technical instruction', that the syllabus in schools needed to be broadened and 'civics' should be taught to all students. So far as teachers were concerned, he argued for a teacher training college for the whole of the West Indies, possibly located in Jamaica, and said that the salaries of teachers should be increased by 50 per cent to ensure that the profession attracted the most appropriate recruits.

Next was Barbados and, here too, Jones impressed its people with his humanity and intelligence, becoming known across the island as 'Great Morgan'.[21] One of the less progressive views held by a number of the commissioners was that poverty was due to an increasing birth rate among the local population. This was not Jones' view, and on one occasion he openly accused his colleagues of engaging in birth control 'propaganda'.[22] He won plaudits from literally all quarters, including the Coptic Orthodox Church of

Ethiopia in Barbados. They saw Morgan as a man who was 'broadminded and unselfish', a man 'of rare accomplishment, choice spirit and sterling character'.[23]

Of all the commissioners, Walter Citrine and Morgan Jones were, in particular, prepared to meet and listen to a broad range of opinion, as was shown by the fact that they had dinner at the home of one of the so-called agitators in Barbados. When Lord Citrine passed away in 1983, the prime minister of Barbados wrote to *The Times* in response to its obituary of the former commissioner. In the letter Mr J.M.G. Adams recalled how, when he was a small boy, Walter Citrine and Morgan Jones had visited his father's house. In the view of the prime minister this was to their credit and the Moyne Commission's report had, said Mr Adams, a significant and positive impact on political progress in the West Indies, leading 'ultimately to the independence of nearly all of Britain's former colonies in the Caribbean'.[24]

Tragically, as the commission was nearing the end of its work in British Guiana, Jones was taken seriously ill, suffering a heart attack. He had experienced a mild heart attack when he was in his early 40s, but this one was much more serious.[25] He was immediately taken to a local hospital but it was felt necessary for him to return to Britain, ahead of the other members of the commission who still had to conclude their work in British Guiana before completing their itinerary in Trinidad. Morgan Jones therefore travelled back to England on the *S.S. Inanda*, a cargo boat, and was met by his wife in Plymouth where the colonial office made special arrangements for him to pass through customs at London.[26]

Morgan Jones' letter to the secretary of state for the colonies. (Courtesy of the National Archives)

After five weeks recuperating in bed at home, Jones wrote a letter on *S.S. Inanda* headed paper to Malcolm MacDonald MP, secretary of state for the colonies and son of Ramsay MacDonald. In the letter, Jones stated that he was now 'very much better', but that the 'autocratic doctors' may not allow him to resume work until 'after Easter'.[27] He bemoaned the fact that he was not able to be with the commission in British Guiana and Trinidad, but hoped to be well enough to play a full part in the consideration of the commission's report. Typically, he expressed his concern that he may have let the commission down, but certainly hoped to be well enough for the Budget on April 26th.[28] This was sadly not to be, because in the early hours of Sunday April 23rd, 1939, Morgan Jones suffered another, and this time fatal, heart attack.

News of his death spread quickly and was greeted with universal shock, not least by those who had been involved with his work in the West Indies. On hearing the tragic news, Malcolm MacDonald wrote to Jones' wife, describing how he had first met her husband when they were addressing a meeting together in Leicester many years previously.[29] The speech Jones had made on that occasion, wrote MacDonald, had won his 'admiration' and he had maintained 'the highest possible regard' for her husband's qualities.[30] As MacDonald had been a Labour MP but had followed his father when he had formed the National government, it was telling that he stated in his letter that Jones had 'never allowed the personal friendship between us to be disturbed by political differences, even at the bitterest moments of those differences'. MacDonald went on express his view of Jones that, 'In politics he was a most fair-minded man, and in personal relations he was a really delightful friend'. The letter concluded with an expression of sympathy from the governor of the Windward Islands.[31]

There followed many more letters of condolence. These included messages from the president of Grenada, the governor's deputy in Jamaica and from trade unions. There were also resolutions passed by legislative councils throughout the region.[32]

The report of the Royal Commission was published in summary in February 1940 and in full in 1945. It contained a number of radical proposals to improve education, communications, public health and the structure of government in Britain's West Indies colonies. The report also contained controversial social proposals, including the recognition of trade unions, and called for a diversification of agriculture and less reliance on sugar production.[33]

Undoubtedly, many of Morgan Jones' progressive opinions and views were reflected in its conclusions and recommendations and, in a note at the beginning of the summary report of 1940, generous tribute was paid to Jones and reference was made to his 'knowledge, sympathy, single-mindedness and unflagging industry'. It even stated that he had 'spent himself in the prosecution of our inquiry into conditions in His Majesty's West Indian possessions'.[34]

In many ways, the Moyne Commission was a turning point in colonial relationships. The view that the uprisings were unprovoked eruptions of discontent was dismissed and, instead, they were seen as an understandable protest at the miserable existence which many had to endure. This would have been Jones' view and there can be no doubt that he made a huge contribution to the work of the Royal Commission. Walter Citrine was of the opinion, however, that being such an active member of the commission had taken its toll on Jones,[35] a view shared by Jones' widow. She said that being a member of the commission was "the most strenuous work he had ever done. It shortened his life".[36] We know from Gladys that her husband was an 'emotionally, highly-strung man who threw himself into whatever public work he did'.[37] Certainly his commitment to the work of the Royal Commission was beyond doubt.

Being a heavy smoker, over many years, of Craven A cigarettes undoubtedly contributed to Jones' premature death,[38] but what he experienced when incarcerated during the First World War also irreparably weakened him. As the *Manchester Guardian* noted in its obituary, the 'privation' he suffered as a conscientious objector 'severely affected his health and it may be said that he never fully recovered'.[39]

Shortly after Jones' death, the members of the Committee of Public Accounts unanimously placed on record their appreciation of his services as committee chair for the previous eight years. They recorded that he had discharged his services 'with conspicuous dignity, ability and impartiality, at the same time inspiring the warmest feelings in all his colleagues'.[40] There was also generous appreciation expressed by the senior Treasury civil servants who were present at the meeting, and who had come to know him well. Sir Herbert Creedy, the senior accounting officer, who knew Jones particularly well, spoke of a sense of 'personal loss' and although, he said, he and the other accounting officers only appeared as witnesses before the 'rather awe-inspiring committee', Jones 'made us feel that he was a friend...The inquisition might have been thorough but it was always very gentle'.[41]

Many tributes were paid to Jones by his parliamentary colleagues. Alderman Arthur Jenkins, MP for Pontypool, spoke for many when he said that Jones' death was 'a great loss to the Labour movement',[42] and the leader of the opposition, Clem Attlee MP accurately said that Morgan Jones' work 'for India and colonial peoples will cause him to be mourned by many outside this country'.[43] Amongst many tributes, the warmest probably came from Jones' close friend Rhys J. Davies MP. He told the *Western Mail* that he would always remember Morgan Jones as 'a man of upright character. He knew his economics and politics as well as most, but he was immersed in spiritual values as well. He never forgot the deeper social problems that in the end determine the destinies of nations'.[44] Rhys J. Davies also referred to the visits he and Jones had made to the United States, saying that whenever they travelled, Morgan Jones' thoughts were 'of his home, his family and the people of Caerphilly'.[45]

The former president of the National Union of Teachers wrote an appreciation of Morgan Jones in the union's newspaper *The Schoolmaster*.[46] Not only did he acknowledge Jones' significant contribution to education, he also wrote movingly about the close friendship they had enjoyed. Dan Edwards, originally from south Wales and who had known Jones for many years, wrote how he had met him for the last time in Llandudno, shortly before his death. To his enquiry about his health, Jones had replied that he 'was better'. Tellingly, however, Dan Edwards wrote 'it pained me to realise he was a sick man, troubled in spirit and weary. I cannot escape the thought that the danger of another world war was too much of a strain for him in his then state of health'.[47]

In Caerphilly and across industrial south Wales many individuals and organisations paid tribute to Morgan Jones. One of the most telling was from John Evans, the clerk to Gelligaer Council. In a lengthy tribute in the *Merthyr Express*,[48] Evans began by describing Jones' early days in Gelligaer and the qualities he brought to the council as a young man. The huge personal qualities of Jones, said Evans, became increasingly evident as he achieved UK-wide prominence. Evans referred to Jones' 'cheeriness and geniality', his strong sense of service, his statesmanship and his fertile mind but, 'perhaps the loveliest characteristic,' wrote Evans, 'was his love for his home, his wife and children, his aged mother and other members of his family whom he cherished so much, and to whom the blow is such a severe one'.[49]

Albert Thomas, the miners' agent in Bargoed, referred to the friendship between himself and Morgan Jones and how his MP used to call at his home and 'talk over his troubles as well as his successes'.[50] Ness Edwards, another local miners' agent, also paid tribute to Jones noting, 'The work he has done in the division will be an everlasting monument to his integrity and his struggle on behalf of the working class", adding that it would be "extremely difficult for a successor to maintain the high standard set by Mr Morgan Jones'.[51] Edwards was, in fact, to be Jones' successor as MP for Caerphilly.

Morgan Jones' funeral, attended only by men, was held in Golders Green crematorium, north London. There was a short service at Jones' home, at which H.B. Lees-Smith, the former president of the Board of Education, said a few words. This was followed by a cremation, attended by a large number of Labour MPs and teachers' representatives, as well as local Labour Party members from the division and members of the Moyne Commission.[52]

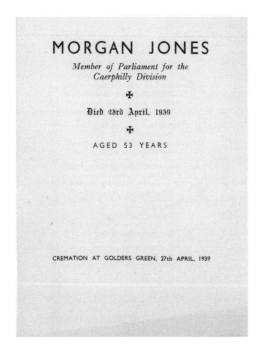

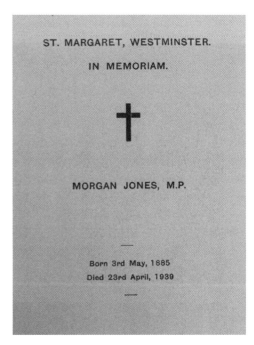

The Order of Service for Morgan Jones'
cremation service in Golders Green.

Front cover of the Order of Service for Morgan
Jones' Memorial Service in Westminster.

Shortly afterwards there was a memorial service at St. Margaret's, Westminster, the church of parliament. This was attended by several members of the cabinet, the leader of the opposition and many MPs of all parties.[53] A little later there were two further memorial services at Baptist churches in the Caerphilly division – one at Hanbury Road Baptist Church in Bargoed, and the other at Tonyfelin Welsh Baptist Church in Caerphilly. At the Bargoed service, tributes were paid by James Griffiths, MP for Llanelli, Jones' close friend Rhys J. Davies MP, the local miners' agent and Morgan Jones' private secretary from when he had been an education minister. At the Caerphilly service a tribute from Clem Attlee was read out and the service was conducted by the pastor of the neighbouring Mount Carmel Baptist Church.[54]

Morgan Jones' death came as a great shock to everyone in the constituency and to his colleagues in Westminster. He could never have been described as a physically strong man and what he went through as a conscientious objector certainly weakened him; one journalist accurately wrote in the mid-1930s that Morgan Jones had "a pale countenance that suggests more than a brief acquaintance with suffering".[55] Nevertheless, he did not give the impression that he was in poor health or likely to have a fatal heart attack.

The Order of Service for the two Memorial Services held in Jones' Caerphilly constituency.

The many generous tributes also demonstrated that Jones was liked and held in enormously high esteem by everyone who knew him, and by many who knew of him. He was extremely hard working and conscientious, even to the point of sometimes overworking. He was also very emotional and felt deeply about all of the many issues he was engaged with. Whether it was a local issue in which he was involved, a national or international cause he was championing, or an injustice he was highlighting, Jones always demonstrated a total commitment to fighting for what he believed was 'right'. At the same time, he always found time for his family and derived huge pleasure and satisfaction from spending time with his wife Gladys and their two daughters. In essence, Morgan Jones was an able, committed and radical parliamentarian who also made time to be a family man. It was surely a tragedy that someone who had such qualities in abundance should have died at the relatively young age of 53.

Notes

1.   *Hansard,* June 14th, 1938, col.103.
2.   Ibid., col.104.
3.   Ibid.
4.   Ibid.

5. *West India Royal Commission 1938-1939* (recommendations), 1940, Cmd.6174, p.7.
6. Ibid.
7. Ken Post, *Arise Ye Starvelings: The Jamaican Labour Rebellion of 1938 and its Aftermath*, (Martinus Nijhoff Publishers, 1978), p.375.
8. *Jamaican Daily Gleaner*, December 1st, 1938.
9. Robert J. Alexander and Eldon M. Parker, 'The Barbados Labor Movement' in *A History of Organized Labor in the English-speaking West Indies*, (Praeger, 2004), p.256.
10. *Jamaican Daily Gleaner*, December 1st, 1938.
11. Ibid.
12. Ibid.
13. Ibid.
14. Ibid.
15. Ibid.
16. West India Royal Commission 1938-1939, op. cit., cmd.6174. pp.6-7.
17. National Archives, Colonial Office – CO 318/439/3.
18. Ibid.
19. Ibid.
20. Ibid.
21. Ibid.
22. Quoted in Nicole C. Bourbonnais, *Birth Control in the Decolonising Caribbean: Reproductive Practice on Four Islands 1930-1970*, 2016, p.84.
23. Letter to Gladys Jones from the Bishop of Coptic Orthodox Church of Ethiopia in Barbados, May 31st, 1938. Personal papers of Margaret Sheaff.
24. *The Times*, February 10th, 1938.
25. Letter from Margaret Sheaff to Wayne David, October 22nd, 2012.
26. National Archives, Colonial Office, op. cit.
27. Ibid.
28. Ibid.
29. Ibid.
30. Ibid.
31. Ibid.
32. Ibid., and personal papers of Margaret Sheaff.
33. 'West India Royal Commission', Cmd. 6174, op. cit., also 'West India Royal Commission'. Statement of Action Taken on the Recommendations, 1945, Cmd. 6656.
34. Ibid., Cmd. 6174. p.7, also letter from Malcolm MacDonald to Gladys Jones, February 27th, 1940. Personal papers of Margaret Sheaff.
35. *Daily Herald*, April 24th, 1939.
36. *Daily Express*, April 24th, 1939.
37. Ibid.
38. Interview with John and Margaret Sheaff, summer 2015.
39. *Manchester Guardian*, April 24th, 1939.
40. Minutes of the Committee of Public Accounts, House of Commons, April 27th, 1939.
41. Ibid.
42. *Daily Mail*, April 24th, 1939.
43. *Daily Herald*, April 24th, 1939.
44. *Western Mail*, April 25th, 1939.
45. Ibid.
46. *The Schoolmaster*, April 27th, 1939.

47. Ibid.
48. *Merthyr Express*, April 29th, 1939.
49. Ibid.
50. Ibid.
51. Ibid.
52. *South Wales Echo*, April 24th, 1939.
53. *The Times*, May 4th, 1939.
54. *Western Mail*, May 1st, 1939.
55. J.T.R. (anon), 'Mr Morgan Jones MP – Facts and Factors in his Career'. Personal papers of Margaret Sheaff.

EPILOGUE

By any yardstick Morgan Jones was a remarkable man. He was a product of his background: his mother gave him huge support and guidance, and, as a boy growing up in a mining community, he saw at first hand injustice, exploitation and poverty, all of which had a profound impact on him. This sense of indignation was given material expression by the practical philosophy of socialism, combined with the moral radicalism of the non-conformist Baptist Church.

Throughout his all-too-short life, Jones lived, both politically and personally, according to the tenets of Christianity and democratic socialism, as expressed by the early Independent Labour Party. Whether it was in the home, in local politics or in parliament, this is what, essentially, made Morgan Jones the man he was. It is also why he had no time for the insurrectionary, revolutionary politics of the Communist Party or the passive, benign politics of the Liberal Party.

Morgan Jones was a man who truly believed in the worth of his work and its contribution towards the creation of a better society. At times, especially in the 1930s, his workload was enormous, and yet he still found time for his beloved family and drew tremendous enjoyment from their company.

The MP for Caerphilly was also a proud Welshman. He spoke 'the language of Heaven' and believed strongly that Welsh patriotism and national identity needed to have political expression. This led him to take the initial steps towards the development of a distinct Welsh education policy when he was an education minister in the first Labour government. Given his strong support for Welsh interests, he was the obvious choice to lead a cross-party delegation to see the prime minister in 1938, arguing for the creation of the post of secretary of state for Wales, nearly 30 years before the post was established. In many ways, therefore, Morgan Jones can be seen to have been one of the early pioneers of political devolution.

He was also a visionary in the education field. In the Labour governments of 1924 and 1929 he was a competent minister, but his real achievement was the quiet, largely unacknowledged work he did during the late 1930s that helped lay the basis for the radical education policies which were introduced after the Second World War. In fact, Morgan Jones' work foreshadowed the path-breaking educational thinking of a later generation when Harold Wilson's Labour government introduced comprehensive education in the 1960s.

Fundamental to Morgan Jones' socialism was his belief in internationalism. As a frontbencher, he took a keen interest in many countries and areas of the world, not least India and Palestine. Jones truly believed in the inherent goodness of human beings, and he continually sought to persuade others that it was always possible to live in peace. During the First World War, he had taken a principled stand against the war as a conscientious objector and had paid a heavy physical and psychological price. Then, through the 1920s and the early 1930s, he did his utmost to argue for meaningful disarmament and for the strengthening of the League of Nations.

The rise of fascism, however, and the failure of reasoned arguments to hold sway, led Jones to question, and then change his long-held pacifist views. For most of his life Jones, like George Lansbury, was a Christian pacifist, but unlike Lansbury, who continued to believe that war and violence could not be justified under any circumstances, Jones reluctantly came to the view that defensive military action was necessary and justified in the circumstances which developed in the 1930s. He became a firm supporter of Clem Attlee and came to believe that it was essential for the League of Nations to assume the credibility and clout to defeat international aggression and uphold international law, through the use of force if necessary.

By the mid-1930s, the experience of the Italian invasion of Abyssinia, the Spanish Civil War and the aggression of Nazi Germany had persuaded Jones that 'absolute' pacifism was not capable of maintaining and advancing peace. He undoubtedly found it extremely difficult to change or modify his long-held belief in pacifism; the memory of the sheer horror and carnage of the First World War could not be pushed to the back of his mind. Nevertheless, he came to the conclusion that there was a need to support the limited use of force to 'defend' peaceable nations from fascist aggression. This made Jones a politician who was not afraid to be pragmatic, so long as he felt it was for a principled reason.

Morgan Jones died on the eve of the Second World War, after spending time in the Caribbean with the Royal Commission on the British West Indies. Had he lived, there can be no doubt that he would have supported Britain's war effort against the Axis powers. The barbarism displayed in Guernica left an indelible mark on Jones, who was, after all, one of the first British politicians to become aware of the horrors of Nazi Germany.

Throughout his political life, Jones was a supporter of the creation of a Jewish homeland and was always seen to be a supporter of the Zionist cause, but he never failed to realise that the Palestinian people also needed their own country. The co-existence of the Jewish and Palestinian peoples was a goal for which he constantly strived.

The unveiling of a commemorative plaque in honour of Morgan Jones in Bargoed, January 2017. Left to right: Nick Sheaff; Margaret Sheaff; author; Cllr. D. Tudor Davies, Mayor of Bargoed Town Council. (Courtesy of author)

During the First World War, Jones had initially been an 'absolutist' objector, in that he had refused to take up arms or do any kind of work which might have helped the war effort. When he was in prison, though, Jones changed his stance and become an 'alternativist'. His deteriorating health influenced his decision, but it is also the case that he constructed a strong argument for his *volte-face*. This argument brought into question the validity of the 'absolutist' argument and lost him some good friends.

Just as Morgan Jones was prepared to do what he believed was right during the First World War, so he was prepared to change his views about pacifism in the 1930s. He accurately believed that it is sometimes more difficult to change your views than it is to maintain them. What was always important for him, though, was that the conclusions he reached were the correct ones, and arrived at for the right reasons.

If Morgan Jones had lived beyond the Second World War, he would surely have been a government minister in the great reforming Labour Governments of 1945-51. He was well respected in the House of Commons and his colleagues in the Parliamentary Labour Party fully recognised his enormous parliamentary workload – on the floor of the House of Commons and in the Public Accounts Committee – during the 1930s. This broad recognition of his worth could have meant, perhaps, that he may well have fulfilled his ambition by becoming speaker of the House of Commons. As it is, Morgan Jones will always be remembered as the first conscientious objector to be elected to parliament, but he should also be known for so much more.

INDEX

A

Aber Valley 8, 67
Aberdare 9
Abergele 19
Abertridwr 8, 52
Abyssinia 79, 83, 107
Adams, J.M.G. 98
Allen, Clifford 15, 21, 23
Andrews, Elizabeth 36
Antigua 93
Arab(s) 86-8
Assherton, Ralph 95
Attlee, Clem 65, 80, 85, 87, 101, 103, 107
Australia 49
Axis powers 83, 107

B

Bahamas 93
Baldwin, Stanley 67
Balfour Declaration 86, 88
Baptist(s) 1-3, 30, 47, 103, 106
Barbados 93, 95-8
Bargoed v, 2-5, 7-8, 10, 13-15, 18, 24-5, 37-9,
    48, 102-3, 108
Barker, Rodney 52
Basque Country 81
Bedlinog 5, 33-4
Bedwas 1, 69-70
Bedwellty 10, 69
Belgium (Belgian) 8-9
Bermuda 95
Bevan, Aneurin 73
Bevin, Ernest 79
Black Friday 31-2
Blackdown Camp (Farnborough) 25
Board of Education vii, 53-5, 57-9, 62, 103
Bolsheviks 24, 32
Brace, William 8, 30
Bridgend 68
British Guiana 93, 95, 98-9
British Honduras 92, 95, 97

Brockway, Fenner 8, 16, 23-4
Brown, Barratt 16
Butler, R.A. 85

C

Caerphilly v, vii, 8-9, 16, 18-9, 31-6, 38, 40,
    45-7, 50, 52, 56, 65, 71, 75, 78-80, 85-6,
    96-7, 101-2, 106
    Miners' Hospital 73
    Parliamentary constituency (division) vi,
        29, 33, 41, 45, 51, 102
    Silver Band 9
    Town Council 67
    Urban District Council (UDC) 10
Caerphilly Journal 3
Camberwell Road 44
Canada 49
Cardiff v, 15-6, 19, 67-9, 73
    Magistrates Court 15
    prison 16, 35
Caribbean 95, 98, 107
Carmel Congregational Chapel 52
Central Labour College 32
Central Welsh Board (CWB) 54-5
Chamberlain, Neville ix, 71-2
Chamberlain, Sir Austen 77-8, 85, 95
China (Chinese) 83, 85
Churt 45
Citrine, Sir Walter 95-6, 98, 100
Cobden, Richard 16
Communist Party (of Great Britain)
    (CPGB) vii-viii, 23, 32-5, 37-9, 51-2,
    55-7, 106
Concordat ix, 66
Conscientious objectors (COs) ('Conshies') v,
    vii, 12, 19, 21, 23, 31, 33, 35, 41, 50, 56,
    86, 100, 103, 107-8
Conservative(s) 3, 33, 56, 65, 67, 77, 80, 95
Coptic Orthodox Church 97
Cory, John 73
Court of the University of Wales 73

Crawford, Helen 34
Creedy, Sir Herbert 100
Cripps, Stafford 65

D
Daily Telegraph 93
Dalton, Hugh 79
Davies, Idris 50
Davies, Rhys J. x, 60, 102-3
Denscombe, Claude 52
Derby Scheme 10
Deri 5, 37
Drake, Barbara viii, 62
Durango 82
Dyffryn House 73

E
Eden, Anthony 82
Edmunds, William Rees 32-3, 35, 37-9
Education Advisory Committee (EAC) viii, 62
Edwards, Charles 10
Edwards, Dan 102
Edwards, Ness 102
Evans, Edgar 34
Evans, John 102
Evans, Revd. D. Leyshon 25
Evian 89

F
Fochriw 5, 52
France 30, 82, 89
Franco, General 81, 82
Freikorps militia 24

G
Gallagher, Willie 34
Gandhi, Mohandas K. (Mahtma) 84-5
Garw Valley 30
Gelligaer 1, 2, 4, 44, 102
    Trades and Labour Council 25
    Urban District Council (UDC) 3-6, 12, 25,
        102
General Strike 50
Geneva ix, 75
George, David Lloyd 1-2, 9, 33, 35-6, 40, 45, 49
Germany (German) ix, 7, 75, 78-9, 81-3,
    87-9, 107
Gilfach Fargoed Boys' School 2
Glamorgan County Council 6, 25, 48, 73
Glamorgan Federation of Teachers 2
Golders Green 44, 82, 102

Grenada 100
Grenfell, Mansel 23
Griffiths, James ix, 72, 103
Guernica (Gernika) ix, 81, 107
Guinness, Walter (1ˢᵗ Baron Moyne) 95, 97-8,
    100, 103

H
Hadow, Sir W.H. 60
Hampstead Garden Suburb 44
Hanbury Road Baptist Church (Bargoed) 103
Hardie, Keir 9
Harris, William 30-1
Henderson, Arthur 33, 39, 79
Hengoed 1, 8, 13
Heol Ddu Isaf 5
Hitler, Adolf 78, 88, 95
Hoare, Sir Samuel 85
Hodges, Frank 30, 56
Hoyes, F.A. 96
Hughes, Emrys 19, 25
Hungary 89

I
Inanda, S.S. 98-9
Independent Labour Party (ILP) vii, 3, 7,
    9-11, 15-19, 22-5, 30, 34, 36, 39, 65, 106
India 84-6, 88, 102, 107
    Congress Party 84-6
    Home Rule League 84
International Federation of Trade Unionists
    (IFTU) 95
Inter-Parliamentary Union (IPU) ix, 75
Italy 76, 79

J
Jackson, Sir Percy 60
Jackson, Tommy 34-5
Jamaican Daily Gleaner 96
Japan 76-8
Jenkins, Arthur 45, 101
Jenkins, Hattie and Roy 45
Jerusalem 49, 88
Jew(s) viii-ix, 50,82-3, 86-9, 107
Jewish Homeland/State 50, 86-8, 107
Jones (*née* Thomas), Gladys 43-6, 100, 103
Jones, Brenda Mair 44-5, 56
Jones, E. 3
Jones, Jack 34-5
Jones, Margaret Eluned 44-5
Jones, Sarah Ann 1, 5, 48

Jones, T.I. Mardy 36, 38
Jones, Thomas 2

K
Kingston (Jamaica) 94-5
Kinmel Park Army Camp 19, 23
Kitchener, Lord 10

L
Labour Leader 16-7, 19, 39
Labour Party vii, ix, 25, 29, 30, 32, 34-5, 38-
    40, 45, 50-2, 55-6, 59-62, 65, 75, 77, 79,
    84-7, 103
    National Executive Committee (NEC) 50,
        55-6, 79
    Parliamentary Labour Party (PLP) v, 71,
        79, 108
Lancashire 25, 60
Lancashire Fusiliers 24-5
Lansbury, George 65, 77, 79, 85, 107
League of Nations ix, 50, 75, 77, 79, 80, 83-4,
    87, 107
Lees-Smith 59, 103
Leeward Islands 97
Lewis School 1-2, 47
Lewis, Edward 3
Liberal Party (Liberalism) 1, 3, 32-3, 37, 39,
    53, 59, 106
Lib-Lab(ism) 3, 86
Liebknecht, Karl 24
Llanbradach 40
Llancaiach Fawr 1
Llandudno 55, 102
Llanfabon 1
Lombard Street 49
London v, viii, 8, 15, 34, 43-5, 47, 49, 54, 65,
    68, 72, 88, 94, 98, 103
Luxembourg, Rosa 24

M
MacDonald, Malcolm 99
MacDonald, Ramsay viii, 30, 33, 53-4, 56-7,
    59, 65
MacMannus, Arthur 34
Macpherson, Ian 36
Madrid 81
Maesycwmmer 8
Manchester v, 36-7
Manchester Guardian 100
Manchuria 76, 78, 83
Mansion House 15-6

Marshall, Catherine 20-1
McLean, John 34
Merthyr Tydfil 9, 11, 32, 36, 43-4
Merthyr Express 9, 37, 54, 102
Merthyr Pioneer 19, 22-5
Military Service Act 10-12, 15
Miners' Federation of Great Britain
    (MFGB) 29-30, 51
Miners' Minority Movement 51
Monmouthshire County Council 29
Morgan, Lieutenant Colonel D. Watts 36
Morris, T.C. 36
Mount Carmel Baptist Church
    (Caerphilly) 103
Mountain Ash 71
Moyne Commission 95, 98, 100, 103
Munich Agreement 95
Mussolini, Benito 79

N
National Association of Labour Teachers
    (NALT) 56
National Council of Labour Colleges
    (NCLC) 55
National Eisteddfod 71
National Liberal vii, 39
National Union of Teachers (NUT) 102
Navigation Colliery 69
Nehru, Jawaharlal 84
Nelson 33
New Fabian Research Bureau (NFRB) 60
Newbold, Walter 23, 34
Newport 68
No-Conscription Fellowship (NCF) 8, 10-11,
    15, 17-9, 20-4
Noel-Baker, Philip 81-2

O
Onions, Alfred 8, 29-30, 32

P
Pacifists, pacifism vii, ix, 35, 79-80, 83-4, 107-8
Palestine 86-9, 107
Parliamentary Committee of Public
    Accounts ix, 65-7, 76, 100, 108
Paul, William 34
Peel Commission 87, 88
Pengam 1, 4-5, 8, 37, 47
Phillips, Morgan 25
Plaid (Genedlaethol) Cymru 71
Plymouth 98

Poland 89
Pollitt, Harry 34
Pontllanfraith 30
Port Talbot 68

R
Reading Normal Training College 2
Reading University 2-3
Rees, Dylan 53, 57
Rhos Cottages 1
Rhymney Valley vii, 1, 3-4, 8, 30-3, 47-8, 50-2, 69
Richards, Tom 8
Risca Urban District Council (UDC) 29
Romania 89
Roosevelt, President 89
Russell, Bertrand 8, 18
Russia 24, 32, 50
Russian Revolution 24

S
Salisbury Group 85
Schoolmaster, The 101
Second World War 62, 86, 106-8,
Senghenydd 8, 67
Sheaff, John v, 44
Simon, Brian viii
Sirhowy Valley 29
Snowden, Philip 30, 45, 57
Socialist(ism) 3, 7, 13-4, 23, 31, 35-6, 50, 52
Soermus, Eduard 24
South Wales Anti-Conscription Council (SWACC) 8
South Wales Miners' Federation (The Fed) 8, 29-30, 70
Spanish Civil War ix, 82, 107
Spencer, George 56
St. Lucia 93
St. Ives (Cornwall) 45
St. Kitts 92-3
Stannard, Harold 93
Stay Down Strike 70
Steer, George 81-2
Stewart, Bob 32, 34-5, 39
Sudetenland 82-3
Sussex 32, 45
Syndicalists 32

T
Taff Merthyr Colliery 69
Taff's Well 33

Tawney, R.H. viii, 52, 62
Teachers' Labour League (TLL) 55-6
Thomas, Albert (Alderman) 30, 102
Thomas-Symonds, Nick 31
Thompson, Brigadier-General 36
Times, The viii, 38-9, 81, 93-4, 98, 101
Tonyfelin Baptist Church 47, 103
Trades Union Congress (TUC) 79, 87, 95-6
Traherne, Sir Cennydd 73
Treharris 33
Trelewis 5, 33, 38
Trevelyan, Sir Charles 53, 55, 57, 59
Tribunal, The 23
Tribunals 11-12, 16
Trinidad 95, 98-9
Triple Alliance 31
Twyn (Y / The) 9, 35, 38

U
United States of America 45, 60, 75, 82, 102

V
Vale of Glamorgan 73
Vaynor 44
Vaughan, Joe 34
Virginia Park 50

W
Wales 1, 3, 6, 8-10, 15, 18-22, 24-5, 29-32, 34, 36, 43, 45, 47, 50-1, 54-5, 59, 65, 67, 69, 71-3, 101
   devolution ix, 71-3, 106
   Welsh language 1, 34, 38, 71, 102, 106
Wallhead, Dick 36
Warwick 19-21, 24
Webb, Beatrice 53
Wedgewood, Josiah 86
Welsh National Council for Education (WNCE) 55
Western Mail 33-6, 39, 47, 59, 78, 100
West Indies 88, 92-3, 95-100, 107
West Riding Education Committee 60
Westhoughton 60
Windward Islands 95, 97, 100
Workers' Educational Association (WEA) 55
Workers' Travel Association 44
Wormwood Scrubs Prison 19-21, 23

Z
Zionism (Zionists) 87, 107

SELECT BIBLIOGRAPHY

1. Primary sources

1.1 Public records
Hansard, Official Record of Parliamentary Debates.

Minutes of Gelligaer Urban District Council (Glamorgan Archives).

Parliamentary Archives, including minutes and correspondence of the Committee of Public Accounts.

Second Industrial Survey of South Wales Vols. I, II and III (University Press Board, Cardiff, for the National Industrial Development Council of Wales and Monmouthshire, 1937).

Union Interparlementaire, Compte Rendu de la XXVIIIe Conférence. 20 au 26 juillet 1932. (I.P.U. Archives, House of Commons).

West India Royal Commission 1938-1939 (Recommendations), 1940, Cmd. 6174.

West India Royal Commission, Statement of Action Taken on the Recommendations, 1945, Cmd. 6656.

1.2 Other Papers
1929 Election Address, from Prof. R. Deacon.

L.S.E. Library, I.L.P. papers, papers of New Fabian Research Bureau.

Letter from Margaret Sheaff to Wayne David, October 2012.

Minute Book of Caerphilly Workmen's Hall and Institute 1926-1928 (courtesy of Hall Committee).

Minutes of Penallta Lodge, Rhymney Valley, in the South Wales Coalfield Collection in the Richard Burton Archives, Swansea. University Library, transcript of interview with Edgar Evans, South Wales Miners' Library.

Museum of People's History, correspondence from Morgan Jones to the general secretary of the Labour Party.

Papers of the Colonial Office (National Archives, Kew).

Personal papers of Margaret Sheaff, including an Appreciation by Rhys J. Davies M.P., recollections of Margaret Sheaff in conversation with Nick Sheaff (2011) and various correspondence and memorabilia.

Shodhganga, Inflibnet Centre, *Activities of the Indian Home Rule League in Britian (1916-1920)*, (anonymous PhD. thesis)

1.3 Interviews
Margaret Jenkins, Caerphilly, summer 2015.

John and Margaret Sheaff, summer 2015

1.4 Newspapers and Journals
Berkshire Chronicle

Daily Herald

Daily Express

Daily Mail

Daily Telegraph	*South Wales Argus*
Jamaican Daily Gleaner	*South Wales Echo*
Labour Leader	*The Schoolmaster*
Manchester Guardian	*The Times*
Merthyr Express	*The Tribunal*
Merthyr Pioneer	*Western Mail*

1.5 Reports

Labour Party, annual conference reports

2. Secondary sources

Alexander, Robert J. and Parker, Eldon. M., 'The Barbados Labor Movement', in *A History of Organised Labour in the English-speaking West Indies*, (Praeger, 2004).

Arnot, R. Page, *South Wales Miners: A History of the South Wales Miners' Federation, 1914-1926*, (Cymric Press, 1975).

Barker, Rodney, *Education and Politics, 1900-1951: A Study of the Labour Party*, (Clarendon Press, 1972).

Bassett, R., *Democracy and Foreign Policy. A case study: the Sino-Japanese Dispute, 1931-1933*, (London School of Economics and Political Science, 1952).

Bourbonnais, Nicole C., *Birth Control in the Decolonising Caribbean: Reproductive Practice on Four Islands, 1930-1970*, (Cambridge University Press, 2016).

Cambridge, Julie, The Caerphilly By-Election of 1921, (Journal of Caerphilly Local History Society, No. 7, 2004).

Cole, G.D.H., *A History of the Labour Party from 1914*, (Routledge and Kegam Paul, 1948).

Craig, F.W.S. *British Parliamentary Election Results: 1885-1918*, (Palgrave Macmillan, 1974).

David, Kay, *The Rhymney Valley and the Great War*, (Lewis Boys Comprehensive School, 1992).

David, Wayne, *Remaining True – A Biography of Ness Edwards*, (Caerphilly Local History Society, 2006).

David, Wayne, 'The Labour Party and the 'exclusion' of the Communists: the case of the Ogmore Divisional Labour Party', *Llafur* (Journal for the study of Welsh Labour History) Vol. III, No. 4, 1995.

Eirug, Aled, *Opposition to the First World War in Wales 1914-1918*, (Unpublished PhD thesis, Cardiff University, 2017).

Eirug, Aled, 'Spies and Troublemakers in South Wales: How British intelligence targeted peace and labour activists in south Wales at the height of the Great War', *Llafur*, Vol. XII No. 1, 2016.

Eirug, Aled, *The Opposition to the Great War in Wales 1914-1918*. (University of Wales Press, 2018).

Eirug, Aled, 'The Security Services in South Wales during the First World War', *Welsh History Review*, Vol. XXVIII No. 4., 2017.

Francis, Hywel and Smith, David, *The Fed: A History of the South Wales Miners in the Twentieth Century*, (Lawrence and Wishart, 1980).

Francis, Hywel, *Miners Against Fascism: Wales and the Spanish Civil War*, (Lawrence and Wishart, 1984).

Gelligaer Historical Society, *Bargoed and Gilfach – A Local History*, (Gelligaer Publishing, 2011).

Gilbert, Martin, *Plough My Own Furrow – The Story of Lord Allen of Hurtwood as told through his own correspondence*, (Longmans, 1965).

Gormy, Joseph, *The British Labour Movement and Zionism 1947-1948*, (Routledge, 1983).

Griffiths, James, *Pages From Memory* (J.M. Dent and Sons, 1969).

Griffiths, Robert, *S.O. Davies – A Socialist Faith* (Gomer Press, 1983).

Gupta, Partha Sarathi, 'The Zionist Lobby in the British Labour Party', (Indian History Congress, Proceedings of the 36th Session, 1975).

Holding Government to Account – 150 years of the Committee of Public Accounts, (House of Commons, 2012).

Hopkin, Deian, 'The Merthyr Pioneer 1911- 1922', *Llafur*, Vol. II No. 4, 1979.

Hopkin, Deian, 'The Rise of Labour in Wales, 1890-1914', *Llafur*, Vol. VI, No. 3, 1994.

Jones, Glyndwr G., *Cronicl Caerffili: a collection of notes relating to Caerphilly's past*, (self-published, 1973).

Jones, Jack, *Unfinished Journey*, (Hamish Hamilton, 1937).

Jones, Morgan, 'Perplexities of a Pacifist', *Labour*, August, 1938.

Jones, Morgan, 'The Problems of the Stateless Jew', *Labour*, August, 1938.

Jones, Morgan, *Whither India*, (Labour Party, February, 1935).

Jones, Thomas, *Rhymney Memories* (Gwasg Gower, 1970).

Klugmann, James, *History of the Communist Party of Great Britain 1919-1924*, Vol. I, (Lawrence and Wishart, 1987).

Lepkin, F.L., *The British Labour Party and Zionism, 1917-1947*, (Unpublished Master Thesis, Simon Fraser University, 1986).

Letters from Bertand Russell, June 1916, reprinted in *The Autobiography of Bertrand Russell*, (Routledge, 2000).

Letters reprinted in *Llafur* (Journal for the study of Welsh Labour History) Vol. I, No. 4, 1975.

Marquand, David, *Ramsay MacDonald* (Jonathan Cape, 1977).

Millman, Brook, *Managing Dissent in First World War Britain*, (Frank Cass, 2014).

Morgan K.O., 'Peace Movements in Wales, 1889-1945', *Welsh History Review*, Vol. X No. 3, 1981.

Morgan K.O., *Re-Birth of a Nation*, (University of Wales Press and Clarendon Press, 1981).

Morgan K.O., *Wales in British Politics*, (University of Wales Press, 1963).

Mowat, C.L., *Britain Between the Wars, 1918-1940*, (Methuen, 1968).

Owen, Nicholas, *The British Left and India: Metropolitan Anti-Imperialism, 1885-1947*, (Oxford University Press, 2007).

Phillips, Morgan, *Morgan Phillips: Labour Party Secretary; Socialist International Chairman*, Morgan D Phillips (Ed.), (Spokesman Books, 2017).

Post, Ken, *Arise Ye Starvelings: The Jamaican Labour Rebellion of 1938 and its Aftermath*, (Martinus Nijhoff, 1978).

Preston, Paul, *We Saw Spain Die: Foreign Correspondents in the Spanish Civil War*, (Constable, 2008).

Rees, Dylan, 'Morgan Jones: Educationalist and Labour Politician', *Morgannwg: The Journal of Glamorgan History*, Vol. XXXI, 1987.

Rees, Dylan, entry in the *Dictionary of Labour Biography*, J. Bellamy and J. Saville (Eds.) Vol. IX, (Palgrave Macmillan, 1993).

Richards, H.P., *Tonyfelin Welsh Baptist Church: 1784-1984*, (self-published, 1985).

Sellwood, Dennis G., Caerphilly Miners' District Hospital 1923-1948, (D.G. Sellwood, 2013).

Sheaff, John, *Morgan Jones – A Memorial*, (unpublished,1986).

Shepherd, John and Laybourn, Keith, *Britain's First Labour Government*, (Palgrave Macmillan, 2002).

Shepherd, John, *George Lansbury: At the Heart of Old Labour*, (Oxford University Press, 2007).

Smith, Dai, *Aneurin Bevan and the World of South Wales*, (University of Wales Press, 1993).

Smith, Ewart, *Lewis' School Pengam – A History*, (Old Bakehouse Publications, 2013).

Stewart, Robert, *Breaking The Fetters*, (Lawrence and Wishart, 1967).

Tanner, Duncan, Williams, Chris and Hopkin, Deian (Eds.), *The Labour Party in Wales 1900 – 2000*, (University of Wales Press, 2000).

The History of Dyffryn House and Gardens, (Glamorgan County Council, 1971).

Thomas, Colin, 'The Red Violinist', *Western Mail*, July 29th, 2017.

Thomas-Symonds, Nick, *Attlee - A Life in Politics*, (I.B. Tauris, 2010).

Who's Who of British Members of Parliament, Vol. III, 1919-1945, (Harvester University Press, 1979).

Williams, Chris, entry in *Oxford Dictionary of National Biography*, (Oxford University Press, 2004).

Williams, Marie A. and Jenkins, Geraint H., *Let's Do Our Best for the Ancient Tongue: the Welsh Language in the Twentieth Century*, (University of Wales Press, 2000).

Zarjevski, Yefim, *The People Have The Floor: A History of the Inter-Parliamentary Union*, (Dartmouth Publishing Co. Ltd., 1989).

welsh academic press

'I picked up this book expecting it to be a hatchet job, but it is a very fair book and a very well researched book. The problem with George Thomas is that one can write a book that is very fair and very well researched yet he still comes out of it very badly.'
Vaughan Roderick, BBC Wales

Award-winning journalist Martin Shipton reveals the real George Thomas and discovers a number of surprising and shocking personae.

978-1-86057-137-4   304pp   £16.99   PB   2017

'Davies's analysis of complex issues is lucid and his narrative is well paced. As such, it's an extremely readable and significant addition to the literature on the Spanish Civil War.'
Morning Star

Almost 200 Welshmen and women volunteered to join the International Brigade and travelled to Spain to fight fascism alongside the Republican government during the 1936-1939 Spanish Civil War. While over 150 returned home, at least 35 died during the brutal conflict. *'You Are Legend'* is their remarkable story.

978-1-86057-130-5   224pp   £19.99   PB   2018

'The full truth about Aberfan'
The Guardian

'The research is outstanding…the investigation is substantial, balanced and authoritative…this is certainly the definitive book on the subject…Meticulous.'
John R. Davis, Journal of Contemporary British History

McLean and Johnes explain how and why the disaster happened and why nobody was held responsible.

978-1-86057-133-6   192pp   £19.99   PB   2019

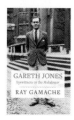

'Excellent … serves as a warning to journalists not to be taken in by official sources and political ideology but to report what they actually learn through their own efforts.'
Prof. Maurine H. Beasley, Univ. of Maryland

Gareth Jones (1905-1934), the Welsh investigative journalist, is revered in Ukraine as a national hero and is now rightly recognised as the first reporter to reveal the horror of the Holodomor, the Soviet Government-induced famine of the early 1930s, which killed millions of Ukrainians.

978-1-86057-122-0   256pp   £19.99   PB   2018

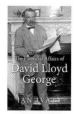

'a cohesive, absorbing account'
J. Graham Jones, from the Foreword

The Financial Affairs of David Lloyd George is the first serious and systematic study to examine, assess and analyse Lloyd George's attitude to money and finance and compellingly illustrates how he accumulated great wealth by fair and more questionable methods.

978-1-86057-125-1   128pp   £19.99   PB   2019

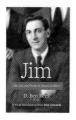

'Ben Rees has crafted a highly-readable and authoritative account of the life and times of one of Wales' greatest statesmen'
Huw Edwards

A product of the Welsh radical political tradition, James Griffiths became a miner at 13 and was a conscientious objector during WW1. He rose to become President of the South Wales Miner's Federation, the MP for Llanelli for 34 years, Chairman and then Deputy Leader of the Labour Party and the first Secretary of State for Wales in 1964.

978-1-86057-120-6   400pp   2019